5/06

Girton;

Happy Reading!

I have a copy too
& found it refreshing.

It is where I was
blessed by a monk on
the Highest mountain in
Chiang Mai, Thailand (the temple
of Doi Suttep).

Laurel

Phra
Borommathat
Doi Suthep
Foundation
Chiangmai

karma

for today's traveler

by Phra Bhasakorn Bhavilai

with David Freyer

karma for today's traveler

A new look at the Buddhist concept of cause and effect, the dazzling processor we call mind, and the fantastic creative power of human intention.

Originally written in Thai by:

Phra Bhasakorn Bhavilai

Re-written and developed in English by:

David Freyer and Phra Bhasakorn Bhavilai

ISBN : 974 - 656 - 846 - 9
1st Edition : Dec 2005
20,000 copies

Printed by : Phra Bhasakorn Bhavilai
Dhammasathan Chiang Mai University
Wat Faihin 67 Mu 1, Ban Faihin, Suthep Rd.
Muang District, Chiang Mai 50200
THAILAND
Tel (66) 053-943684

Printed : Nuntapun Printing Co., Ltd.
33/4-5 Chiang Mai - Hangdong Rd.
Muang District, Chiang Mai 50100
THAILAND
Tel. (66) 053-804908-9

Cover painting : *Reach Doi Suthep - Reach Arahant*
by Chansilp Jaikom

Phra Bhasakorn and David welcome any feedback to Dhammasathan, at the above address and phone.

Foreword

I feel it a privilege to write a foreword to Ven. Bhasakorn Bhavilai's book on the workings of Karma and the human mind. I have enjoyed reading it quite a lot because in it I find something new and thought-provoking.

The law of karma, being one of the most basic and important teachings of the Buddha, has been a favourite topic of hundreds of books by Buddhist scholars. But it seems to me most, if not all, interpretation and presentation have strictly followed the traditional and conservative approach of Theravada Buddhism especially the classic division of Karma into 12 types of the great commentator Buddhaghosa in his authoritative work Visuddhimagga.

The Buddha's teachings including the doctrine of Karma are based on natural truths which are timeless and universal. No one can change them. But ways and means to expound them need not remain the same through ages. Human intellect and knowledge grow along with time and social environment. A means of explaining and presenting the same truth may prove a success in one age but a complete failure in another. That is why the method of presenting a truth or truths is to be improvised all along in order to suit the intellectual and educational backgrounds of the audience. This is where Ven. Bhasakorn's book is relevant.

The Ven. author has tried to explain the workings of Karma and of the human mind in a new way and to make the way accord with the scientific law of the uniformity of nature called World Equilibrium by the author. His clear exposition and graphic illustration may help the student of Buddhism to easily grasp the working of Karma in the life stream of a being. It must not be forgotten that the working of Karma is listed as one of the four "unthinkables" (Acinteyya) because of its intricacy and profundity.

But, I am sure, since science and Buddhism are to carry out the same task of addressing natural truths, so they are complementary; scientific discovery will help verify Buddhist truths as it has already done in such cases as the evolutionlike growth of mankind, the structure of the universe, the gradual growth of the embryo in the womb, etc.

There are still many other subjects in Buddhism that are still open to controversy such as rebirth, other types of beings in the universe, other realms of beings, the nature of Nirvana, the true meaning of anatta, the miracles, etc. These subject matters should be explained in the light of science and presented to the open-minded audience.

I really appreciate the Ven. author's brave venture in presenting his new approach to the interpretation of the profound and problematic teaching of the Buddha. He may meet criticism from some conservative circles as new interpretations of religious doctrines are usually prone to, but I would like to suggest the Ven. author to go ahead with his good work of noble cause with my all-out moral support.

Saeng Chandngarm
Professor Emeritus
Mahamakut Buddhist University
Lanna Campus, Chiang Mai

Chiang Mai, Thailand
November 19, 2005

David's comments

My name is David Freyer. I am a 43 year-old American, and had the good fortune to be raised in a stable, loving family. I was a university honor student in mechanical engineering, worked for a short time in the aerospace industry, then left America to see something of the world. My travels eventually lead me to reside in Thailand where I have lived happily for some years now with my Thai partner.

I met Phra Bhasakorn about five years ago at a university for Buddhist monks, where I teach English, and where he was a Master's Degree student. His energy, directness, humor, and sense of purpose intrigued me immediately. After class he often sought me out to practice explaining, in plain words and drawings on bits of paper, the workings of karma.

His main point was that the workings of karma were often misunderstood, and that if we looked at the world and the mind separately, it might clarify things.

A few years later he had produced a book, in Thai, called Balance of World, Balance of Mind. It was a conversational sort of book, based on the talks he had given on the subject. He told me that he wanted my help to create an English version.

Since I cannot read Thai, and though I teach in a Buddhist university, I am not a Buddhist scholar, it seemed a tall task. Yet Phra Bhasakorn was insistent and I was very interested.

And so we began. Meeting twice weekly in two hour sessions, he began to bring me up to speed. Slowly, patiently, he answered all my questions. He maintained that karma was nothing strange, merely natural law, which, like physics, could be understood. I looked for holes in the logic. He welcomed all my questions, many of which surprised him. I got logical answers and I enjoyed our sessions immensely. During this effort to make things clear to me, we began to appreciate differences in language, understanding, and cultural heritage. We realized that the Thai book could not simply be translated, because it was written for a Thai Buddhist reader. It would have to be rewritten more or less from the ground up, to present the same ideas to a western reader.

Our twice weekly sessions continued, and this book is the result. The writing style is mine; the approach to Buddhist teaching, the meaning, and the content are all Phra Bhasakorn's.

I dedicate the merit I may receive for this book to my wonderful mother and father.

Acknowledgments

This book – *Karma for today's traveler*, which is a translation and improvement from my book in Thai called *Balance of World, Balance of Mind*, is the result of the kind help from many people.

First I would like to pay homage to my Lord Buddha who revealed the truth of nature, the *Dhamma*, to this confused world, and all the desciples, the *Sangha*, who have followed and protected these valuable teachings from the time of the Buddha until now.

Next I would like to thank and pay my respect to my venerable teacher the Buddhist nun Piengduen Tanasanpipit who raised me like a mother into the world of Buddhism.

I would like to give a special thanks to Prof. Dr. Khunying Payom Singhasaneh for financial support, and Miss Athicha Xanthavanij who urged me to translate *Balance of World, Balance of Mind* into English and found me volunteers to translate the book, namely Miss Naruporn Arunpraphan and Ms. Roongtiwa Patrathiranond. A futher thanks goes out to Mr. Suddhinand Janthagul and Assoc. Prof. Sommai Premchit who provided me with two more translations to work from.

For the pictures decorating the book I would like to thank Paulsilpa Rattanachudech, Ekarit Boontharik, Santi Thammarat, Pradit Wanna, Ohm Ratchawet, and Chansilp Jaikom.

As the book was taking shape, many people read through the manuscript offering valuable critiques and suggestions. A big thank you to Prof. Dr. Rawi Bhavilai, John and Kanokwan Cadet, Prof. Saeng Chandngarm, Kristin Foxlee, Jace Hobbs, Scott McGregor, Dr. Anatole-Roger Peltier, and Elizabeth Scribner.

Phra Bhasakorn Bhavilai
Dhammasathan, Chiang Mai University

Chiang Mai, Thailand
December 28, 2005

What's really going on?

All my life I have been interested in two worlds. The world around me and the world inside me. Both appear to follow orderly rules, some kind of cause and effect, yet for years I couldn't seem to get a handle on what those rules actually were. The exacting, reductionist approach of science offered many answers, but my own experiences, feelings and perceptions seemed to occur in a world about which science had little to say. I mean, what did science tell me about my happiness or the ache in my heart? Being born into a Buddhist family, I was familiar with many teachings illustrating the law of cause and effect, the law of karma, yet many of those teachings were difficult for me to grasp, and some even added to my confusion.

Allow me to introduce myself; my name is Phra Bhasakorn and I am a Buddhist monk from Thailand. I was born into an intellectual Buddhist family and was a layman until the age of 35. I studied physics at university and then worked for ten years as a professional photographer. I had my own photography studio in Bangkok, where, as an urban professional I gained valuable experiences about life, achievement, and myself. Big questions about life, the world around me, and the world within me, sent me looking for big answers. In time this quest grew more important for me than my mundane professional life, and it led me deeper and deeper into Buddhism. The approaches and answers that I found there changed my life. Finally I gave away my business and donned the saffron robes. I have been a monk now (2005) for ten years.

The questions I asked appeared simple, like those of a child; If doing good means good comes back to me, and doing bad means bad comes back to me, why do bad things happen to good people? And why do bad people often seem to have very good lives? How can these things happen in a just world? Does good really beget good? What is really going on?

And what about intention? The thought behind the action? Certainly intentionally doing bad is worse than accidentally doing bad. Yet how does it all work? Are there some divine bureaucratic bookkeepers recording all of our actions and intentions throughout our lives, entering the information into some great karmic ledger? And, if so, knowing how quickly our thoughts can shift from good to bad and back again, the bookkeepers must be quite busy. The physics part of me found these angelic accountants very dissatisfying.

To complicate matters further, Buddhism also talks about seemingly minor actions having enormous consequences that appear to defy balance and logic. For example, if you have ever been to Thailand you have no doubt seen barefoot Thai monks in orange robes walking along the street at sunrise. Thai lay people come out to fill the monks' alms bowls with their daily food, thereby making merit for themselves.

Many devout Thais believe that if a person is lucky enough to offer food to an enlightened monk, an Arahant, the merit will be huge. How huge? It is said that the offering of one portion of food into the alms-bowl of an Arahant will be rewarded with many future lives born in material comfort. How is this possible?

When I was a layman, and had not yet been ordained a monk, I did not understand this, and slanderously thought that the Buddha might have been worried about his disciples, thinking that they would face privation. Thus, I thought, he made up a story to encourage people to offer food to his disciples, saying that they will earn merit by this way. I am now convinced that I was wrong. I now believe that the one-portion-of-food-equals-many-comfortable-lives equation is actually true, and if you bear with me for a while I will try to show you why.

I would like to begin with a story, well-known to Buddhists, that illustrates some of the perplexing questions of karma. We shall return to this story throughout the book.

The Story of Angulimala

During the time of the Buddha there was a brilliant student from a wealthy family called Ahimsaka. The other students were jealous of him and eventually managed to turn his teacher* against him. As a result, in order to get rid of him, his teacher made the outrageous demand that to receive the high teaching that he desired, Ahimsaka must first kill one thousand people!

Amazingly, Ahimsaka did not at this point give up, but he continued to trust his teacher, trusting that this shocking demand must somehow be for the overall good. So he set out to complete his task. Ahimsaka became a murderer, lurking in a forest and killing people.

---

* The teacher was not a follower of the Buddha.

3

But keeping count of so many victims is difficult, especially as his murderous action filled his mind with hatred and delusion. So finally, to stay organized and keep track of his progress, he began to cut off the little fingers of his victims, and strung them in a gruesome growing garland which he wore around his neck. This earned him the infamous nick-name Angulimala, which means *finger garland*.

One fateful day, when he had 999 fingers around his neck, there was a convergence of events. The local king, tired of the murderer in the forest, organized his troops to sweep the forest and put an end to Angulimala. At the same time, Angulimala's mother realized that it was her son who was the terrible killer. Yet despite the fact that he was a mass murderer, her motherly love compelled her to go into the forest to warn him about the king.

Angulimala, his mind twisted by his murderous deeds, failed to recognize his own mother and was preparing to kill her to complete his tally when the Buddha intervened.

The Buddha positioned himself between Angulimala and his mother, and Angulimala shifted targets, and began to chase the Buddha. But then something strange happened – even though the Buddha was only walking calmly and unhurriedly, and Angulimala was running with all his might, he still couldn't catch the Buddha. Finally in exasperation Angulimala screamed at the Buddha to stop.

Still walking serenely the Buddha calmly said, *I have stopped but you haven't*. This confused and enraged Angulimala even more and he screamed again for the Buddha to stop and explain what he meant. At this point the Buddha stopped, turned to Angulimala and said that he had already stopped. He had stopped killing and harming other living beings and it was time now for Angulimala to do likewise. These words struck Angulimala with such force that he dropped his weapons, followed the Buddha back to his monastery and became a monk.

Not knowing that the killer was now a monk, the pious king came with his troops to pay respect to the Buddha before heading into the forest to find Angulimala. The Buddha asked the king what his reaction would be if he learned that the infamous killer was now a monk in this very monastery. The king, unable even to imagine such a vile, murderous beast as a monk and follower of the Buddha, answered that if it was indeed true, he would pardon him of his crimes and pay him the respect due a monk. The Buddha then pointed and said there sits Angulimala.

Once the king overcame his shock and fear, he kept his word, paid respect to the new monk and said to the Buddha, "What we had tried to do by force and with weapons, you have done with neither."

Shortly thereafter, following the Buddha's teaching, the former mass murderer Angulimala became an Arahant, that is to say, he attained enlightenment.

Then for some time, when the enlightened Angulimala would walk near the local people, stray rocks and sticks, thrown by villagers, would strike him in the head injuring him, and causing him to bleed. It is said that these 'accidental' injuries were from his karma coming back to him, from his past actions as a mass murderer.

So what do you think? Did Angulimala get away with murder? Is it fair for his victims that he walks free? Is it right that after killing a thousand people his only payback is a few head wounds – because he had become enlightened? Do his minor injuries balance the scales of justice against a thousand murders and grieving relatives? Years ago I could not imagine how such an outcome could be considered fair. Yet now I can see the fairness.

Let's bring it a little closer to home. Think back to some horrible, cruel murder that made the headlines in recent years. If the guilty person were suddenly to announce: "I am now enlightened. I should not be punished or imprisoned any longer to repay my past bad deeds." Would we agree to let the killer go scot-free?

Even if we suppose it was actually true, that the killer had indeed become enlightened, would that change our minds? Or would we think something along the lines of – congratulations for your spiritual progress, but your victims are still dead, so you must continue to sit in prison. Imagine further that the victims were our friends or relatives. Surely we would not tolerate to have the killer walk free, enlightened or not. So how to reconcile the story of Angulimala? If bad begets bad, what happened to all of that bad karma? When I was a young layman, the story of Angulimala perplexed me.

The big question in my mind was basically this: How do our personal actions and intentions come back to affect us? To me it seems like a key question. As a young layman, I felt that until I understood how my own actions and intentions would impact my own life, there was no rational way to organize my efforts or set my goals. So I set out to find some answers.

Being ordained as a Buddhist monk afforded me the time and resources necessary to research the Buddhist teachings. This little book is my attempt to share with you some of what I have found. It is a book about cause and effect. A book about karma. The first part will deal with our external world, while the second, more important part, will deal with our internal world. The final chapter contains my own thoughts on the evolution of mind.

Intention and action

The Buddhist teachings say that all effects have causes and that all things are conditioned by the causes that produced them. Furthermore, this chain of events is rational and its workings can be understood. Indeed, Buddhist teaching states that karma is one of the laws of nature, like gravity and electromagnetism.

So let's begin with the basics, the ABC's of cause and effect according to Buddhism. Just like combinations of letters become words and sentences, combinations of behaviors create karma.

1) Intention leads to action:

When we reflect on our normal behavior we find that most of our actions start from *intention*. We have an intention and then we *act*. We hold this book in our hands and think that it may be interesting to read, so we decide to open it and we open it. Our thought leads to action. By action I mean all bodily and verbal action.

2) Action without intention:

For our second category we have those times when we act without conscious intention. For example, suppose we're driving a car and hit and kill a man who stepped into the road. We tried to stop but we could not. It was not our intention to kill him, yet he is dead. Do we have to suffer consequences? Certainly. Our car is damaged, the police will question us, a judge may decide that we were driving carelessly or too fast. We may be fined or imprisoned, or troubled by a terrible memory.

Let's look at another example. We go on a picnic, eat a banana, throw the banana peel into the forest and go home. However, our banana peel fell onto a forest path that we did not see. A sweet old lady slips on our banana peel, cracks her head and dies. As for us, our life goes on, we forget all about the banana. The lady remains dead. Our unintended action plays a part in her death. Thus even small, unintended actions may have large results.

Throughout our life, we cannot know how many sweet old ladies might have died from slipping on our banana peels. Did we have any intention of causing harm with our banana? Of course not, but the fact remains that someone died, and our unintentional action was involved.

3) Intention without action:

For our final category of karma we have those times when our intention leads to no bodily or verbal action. Thoughts are constantly arising in our everyday life and our various intentions are changing countless times, moment by moment. Many, many thoughts arise and pass without our taking action. These thoughts can affect our physiology – a happy memory cheers us, a sad memory depresses us – but for now, let's limit our concept of *action* to bodily and verbal action in the *external* world. And let our external world include our physical environment, the people around us, and society.

So we have three categories of intention and action:
1) Intention leads to action
2) Action without intention
3) Intention without action

If we put the intention on the left and the action on the right we get the chart below. On the intention side we can see that there are two mind effects, and on the action side there are two world effects.

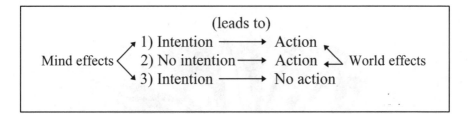

The *mind effects* are things that disturb or clarify our minds, things that bring us mental suffering or mental joy, serenity or sadness. Every thought we have, whether acted upon or not, has an effect on our mental environment. This cause and effect link is natural law at work. It is unavoidable and inexorable.

Our good thoughts benefit us and our bad thoughts hurt us. This latter, often overlooked fact, is the cause of much suffering in the world. We will look at this mental activity in the second part of the book.

The *world effects* are more straightforward. They are the sum of all bodily and verbal actions and their effects on our world. In our chart we see that there are two cases of acting – that due to intention and that without intention.

Both always have a direct effect on our environment, and since all things are interconnected, these effects always have further effects, however small. These chains of effects go on and on through time. In Thailand we have a saying "plucking a flower and affecting a star."

World Equilibrium

To begin with, I would like to discuss our external world – a world with which we are in constant interaction. Imagine yourself floating in a very large, calm pool. Every motion that you make causes ripples and movement of the water. You simply cannot move without the water reacting to your movement. And when the water moves, you are in turn affected by the current and waves. You and the water are in an interconnected balance. That's more or less the situation we are in; all our actions change or disturb our environment, and all changes or disturbances in our environment affect us.

In this fully-connected environment, a single action does not produce a single effect. For example, if we move our hand through the water, we create not a single wave, but many small waves. One action creates a multitude of waves. All these waves go out into our environment, and through our environment we receive each of their echoes as feedback.

That's not to say that the best we can do is float motionless, afraid to disturb anything. Non-action is neither sensible nor possible. In reality our pools are not so calm. Things are happening. There are waves and currents and we must react. Living in the world always requires action. The idea is to be wise enough to act in a way that reduces or eliminates reactions that bring us suffering.

So whenever we act, the world reacts, responding in equal measure to the change we impose upon it. A big, sudden action makes a big, sudden change to the world. A slow steady action makes a slow and steady change. All these changes sooner or later feed back to us.

If our actions make changes to the world that are gentle, comfortable and smooth, the world will respond to us in the same gentle manner. Conversely, if our actions are aggressive, hostile and rough, we will receive aggression, hostility and roughness from the world. In a world of instant karma we could illustrate this type of feedback with the diagram below. (I represent mind and body together with a heart-point. For Thais the heart and mind are one, not separated. A Thai person may say 'my mind is calm' and tap his or her chest. So I will continue in the Thai way, with the heart and mind as one.)

an instant karma world

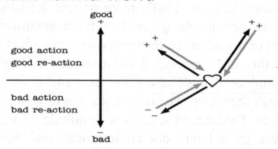

good
+

good action
good re-action

bad action
bad re-action

bad
−

In our instant karma world good begets good and bad begets bad; what comes around goes around; as you sow so shall you reap. Yet, it's not an instant tit for tat, do this get that world. Our picture is not quite right.

Life is a journey through time. From moment to moment time is moving on and our life moves along with time. When we act, it will take some period of time to affect the world. Change requires time. The effect takes time to manifest and the result that feeds back to us will not be instantaneous, but will be experienced in a future moment, when the conditions are right.

karma takes time

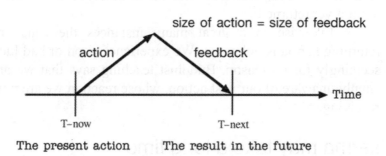

size of action = size of feedback

action   feedback

Time

T-now   T-next

The present action   The result in the future

To illustrate the principles of karma I have shown our action and the returning feedback as single arrows. In fact, the reality is more complex – a continuous interaction of many waves – but the principle is the same: All that we send out, will in some way, shape or form, return. And this process takes some interval of time.

So we must wait for our kindness to return to us. Likewise with our bad action. But, at some point in time, in equal measure to all change imparted to our environment, the results will return. The chickens will come home to roost. No one gets away with anything. We are the owner of our ripples and waves. It is a law of nature. It is fair.

We have all had experiences in our lives where, doing good obtained for us a good result at a future time. Perhaps we were diligent in studying and then did well on an exam, or we spoke nicely with others and had them respond in kind. Certainly we've all experienced that doing bad begets bad as well – teasing a dog and getting bitten, saying unkind words and being repaid with the same.

But what about the good-deed people who get nothing good in return? In the Buddhist view, the conditions for the feedback from the world are not yet in place, so their karma has not yet returned.

Likewise in a great many instances the cause of returning karma is unknown. We experience good or bad luck seemingly for no reason. Buddhist teaching says that we are simply unaware of our past action, whose reaction we are now receiving.

karma may take a long time

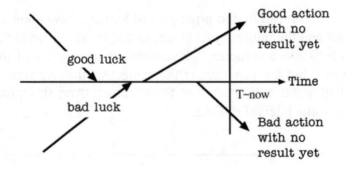

the coming and going of karma

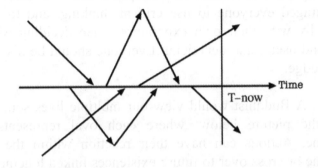

Thus, Buddhists would say that winning the lottery is actually not a case of random luck, but is feedback from our previous actions returning to us – the result of our own intention in a forgotten past. These past actions still resonate in our world, affecting our World Equilibrium.

Suppose we were to die suddenly tomorrow and the results of our good and bad actions had not yet ripened. These actions do not just vanish. Just as energy can neither be created nor destroyed, merely transformed, so too with the effects of our karma. According to Buddhism, our responsibility for our actions does not end with our death. Our ownership of our actions continues beyond this lifetime.

Buddhist doctrine says that we are responsible for our actions through more than this single life. We are responsible until we finally move beyond the playing field of birth and death, until we reach the point that we are free.

If the idea of past and future lives is strange for you, then perhaps you could play along as a mental exercise. Ponder the possibility and consider the ramifications. The Buddha always warned people not to believe what he, or anybody for that matter, said simply because he said it. He encouraged everyone to use critical thinking, and to check carefully with their own experience when deciding what is true and useful and beneficial. Everyone should be his or her own judge.

A Buddhist would view our multiple lives something like the picture below, where each oval represents one lifetime. Actions can have their reaction within the same lifetime or cross over to future existences linked together like a chain by karma.

a chain of lifetimes

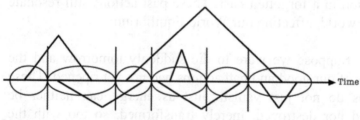

Linking of actions and reactions

Our present life is a short span when compared with the effects of karma. However, this is not to say that we are helpless victims of our old karma. Quite the contrary, this means that we are truly the makers of our own fate; architects of our own environment. Our actions are meaningful. We have the power to make things better. There is nothing random or haphazard about the workings of the universe.

The effects of our karma also lead us to be born in fortunate or unfortunate circumstances. The good fortune to be born with a healthy body into a financially stable, loving home is the result of good past actions. This good fortune may resonate through an entire lifetime, protecting us, insulating us, to some degree, from the rough seas of the world around us. Children from loving, stable families find doors open to education and financial opportunity. Likewise, a less fortunate birth may cause us to suffer and struggle our whole lives for things that others receive freely; yet we are still fortunate to be born human at all.

A word of caution here. The action of karma *does not* mean that we should disregard others' suffering as they are merely *getting what they deserve*. Absolutely not. Such a view lacks compassion and understanding. Buddhist teachings say that in our long chain of lives we have all had experience being rich and poor, beautiful and ugly, happy and sad. And as Jesus said, we have all been sinners. We are all here together in this world, unable to avoid suffering, old age and sickness. Death awaits us all. And since we cannot look back through our lives to see all our past connections and actions, and how they might relate to the person standing in front of us, we should always try to view all beings with compassion and loving kindness.

So what to do?

So what are we to do at this point in a long chain of lifetimes? Our unknown past awaits to ambush our future. We could have a terrible traffic accident, lose our job, or suddenly become ill, all for actions that occurred prior to this life. Indeed the law of cause and effect insists that our past bad actions are echoing through our world, literally accidents waiting to happen. And, Hollywood movies notwithstanding, we cannot go back in time to undo our previous bad deeds.

How can we cope with such a situation where unknown, forgotten retribution lurks in every life? The Buddha advised us not to despair, but rather to understand how karma operates and take action to take control of our lives *now*. There is much we can do.

First, a properly lived present will not create any future bombs to shatter our peace. So we should stop doing bad things. Next, since all the good we do shall return to us, we should start doing more good. Further, the Buddha counseled us to build a wall which prevents us from causing more trouble for ourselves. A wall of harmonious action. A wall of morality. This wall is built by accepting precepts which are strong intentions not to harm ourselves and others.

In fact this wall does more than stop bad action in the present, it actually buffers the effects of the bad actions returning to us. We'll talk more about this buffering effect later. First let's look at this wall.

The Wall of World Harmony

The Buddha taught that the basis of human morality lies in five precepts:

Refrain from killing
Refrain from stealing
Refrain from sexual misconduct
Refrain from lying
Refrain from using intoxicants

By keeping these five precepts one lives in a way that no intentional harm is done either to ourselves or to the world; no hostile, aggressive waves are generated in our sea of world equilibrium. And when no harm is done to the world, the world will have no new harmful feedback for us.

Now let's look at the law of cause and effect and see why we have to observe the five precepts.

The 1st precept: Harmonious conduct regarding Life – if we harm other life, we will be harmed in the same degree. All beings love their lives and want to live. So just as we would like to live unmolested, we should refrain from injuring others or taking life, any life. One who keeps the first precept will not swat a mosquito – he or she would literally not hurt a fly.

The 2nd precept: Harmonious conduct regarding Property – if we do not steal or damage others' property then we will never have to compensate for it. People who have things stolen from them are being paid back in kind from past action against the property of others.

The 3rd precept: Harmonious conduct regarding Sexual Conduct – this deals with socially accepted norms and respect for one another. We must remember that we are all someone's son or daughter, someone's loved one, brother or sister. Our behavior, especially regarding sexual conduct, must be respectful, honorable and careful not to disturb the web of social relations. If criticism about sexual misconduct arises, it will spread quickly disturbing the social equilibrium.

The 4th precept: Harmonious conduct regarding Verbal Action – we should speak only what is true. This will make our world cleaner and more stable. Truthfulness also involves two other important matters: trustworthiness and power. A person who has good verbal behavior keeps his or her word and can be trusted. A promise from such a person is reliable.

Truthfulness is an important source of personal power and has many good effects. Most Buddhist chants originated from stories as told by Arahants, Bodhisatvas (Buddhas-to-be), or the Buddha himself. The chants are effective and have power because they are true.

The 5th precept: Harmonious conduct regarding Mindfulness – simply put, intoxicants decrease mindfulness. If someone is drunk they can break other precepts, doing things that they would never do while sober. Therefore, according to Buddhist doctrine, drugs and alcohol should be avoided.

The question is often raised: "Is it wrong to drink a little if one does not get drunk?" In fact, one who keeps the five precepts will try not to drink at all, because drinking reduces mindfulness, and as mindfulness decreases, destruction increases.

If someone establishes themselves firmly in the five precepts it is very unlikely that they will cause harm to their world equilibrium or themselves. They will act with respect towards life, property, social norms regarding sexuality, truth and mindfulness. Such a person practices harmlessness. Consequently the five precepts can be regarded as a form of 'world protection' because they are conducive to harmonious two-way interaction with the world around us.

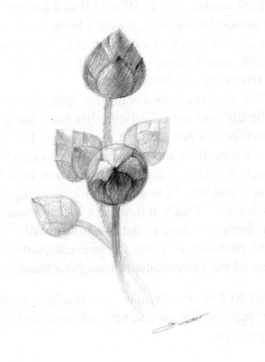

Keeping the wall firm

While few would argue with the sensibility of the five precepts, actually keeping them can sometimes be a problem. I know how hard it can be. When I was a layman I sometimes found it almost impossible. I would begin with a firm resolve and then later in the day I would meet a friend who invited me for a drink and I thought, oh well, why not, and precept number five went out the window.

Yet in fact, observing the precepts is to observe normal bodily and verbal actions. It's quite natural when you think about it. It's not extreme in any way. But how to do it? How can we be firm and stable in the precepts? Because it's not enough to just go through our day, and then look back in the evening and say, "Oh good, I didn't end up breaking any precepts today." That's not what I mean about keeping the precepts firmly. I mean that we must make a conscious, deliberate decision to keep the precepts, and maintain our awareness of our commitment throughout the day.

When I was a layman, my teacher, a venerable nun named Piangduan Dhanasarnpipit, advised me how to observe the five precepts.

On waking up in the morning, she advised me to reflect on the virtues of that which I hold sacred. For me that is the Buddha, his teachings, and those who follow the teachings (In Buddhism this is known as the Triple Gem – the Buddha, the Dhamma, and the Sangha). You may reflect on Jesus, Saint Mary, Mother Earth, Divine Spirit, The I Am – whomever or whatever it is for you that is virtuous and sacred. Then, with your mind filled with this sacred presence, commit yourself to the observance of the precepts. For me, I held my Buddha amulet and said to myself: "Buddha, Dhamma, Sangha, the first precept is refraining from killing, the second precept is refraining from taking what is not given, the third precept is refraining from sexual misconduct, the fourth precept is refraining from false speech and the fifth precept is refraining from taking intoxicating things. I am Mr. Bhasakorn and I now have the intention to observe these five precepts. By the power of these precepts, I make my request: 'May I have a good, smooth, and happy relationship with everyone I contact for business and may my business be successful.'" This little habit of asking for something made it easier and more fun for me to keep the precepts. But it's not just a trick. You get a direct benefit from your precepts.

If you are a student, you may make a request like this: "Today, I have an exam. I may need to make a few guesses. By the power of the precepts, may I guess correctly." I'm not kidding. The power of the precepts can help you succeed. Try it for yourself to see if it works.

Of course, since we are human, after committing to keep the precepts, we may unintentionally forget and break one, like telling a little lie. In other words, we've made a negative impact on our world. When that happens we should remind ourselves of our intention and re-commit ourselves. Other times we may even break a precept intentionally. Afterwards we should remind ourselves again, and once more firmly make the commitment to keep the precepts.

As my observance of the precepts became stronger, yet while I was still a layman, my friends continued inviting me out for an occasional drink. And at times, depending on the social situation, and my own, shall I say, weakness, I still found it difficult to refuse. So I reminded myself of my strong intention to keep the first four precepts and excused myself temporarily from the fifth thusly: "Buddha, Dhamma, Sangha; the first precept is refraining from killing, the second precept is refraining from taking what is not given, the third precept is refraining from sexual misconduct, the fourth precept is refraining from false speech, but the fifth precept - refraining from taking intoxicating things - I have to neglect for a moment." Then, during the social time with my friends, I took extra care not to break any of the remaining four precepts. Once the drinking session with my friends was over, I committed myself to re-observe the fifth precept again.

It may seem strange to you to drop a precept like that when temptation arises, but at that time my resolve was not yet firm enough, and keeping four precepts is much better than keeping none!

My teacher also advised me to repeat my intention of observing the precepts before going to bed at night. Since we cannot break any precepts while we sleep, we can be happy that for roughly one third of our life we can maintain the precepts with no effort at all. And re-affirming our intention to observe the precepts before we go to sleep is a pleasant, easy way to firm-up our resolve, which will help us the next day.

Concentration brings wisdom

Having concentration on keeping the precepts means that we concentrate on our bodily and verbal conduct to evaluate whether our action is wholesome or not. Having the precepts means we have a strong intention not to harm ourselves or others. If we find that our conduct is not proper, we must remind ourselves of our commitment, again and again as necessary. Concentration here means our mind is focused and concentrated on a certain object. In this case, precept-observance is the object of attention. According to Buddhist doctrine, this concentration on keeping the precepts results in wisdom.

What is the nature of wisdom in keeping precepts? Well, for example, after a period of time when we are concentrating on speaking only the truth, we may notice our life becoming smoother and cleaner. We are less encumbered and have more freedom and energy, because we no longer waste any time or energy or words trying to maintain the illusion of the unreal. After all, isn't that what lying is? – an attempt to make what is unreal appear real to another? It takes effort to maintain a lie. Lying steals our freedom. So, in observing the fourth precept we come to notice and understand deeply the nature of false speech. The concentrated effort expended to maintain the fourth precept is thus repaid to us in wisdom.

Practicing the precepts brings mindfulness

With accumulated practice, our precepts will become more developed and our concentration in keeping precepts will become second nature. This will result in a wise attentiveness that keeps us from being careless. This is mindfulness.

Mindfulness is a kind of instant wisdom that makes us aware in each situation what we should do and should not do to avoid any bad conduct and the breaking of precepts. Mindfulness is a preventive device that keeps us from unwholesome action. It is a carefulness and an awareness.

We should always try to be aware of, and have respect for, life, property, society, truth, and mindfulness. Right conduct in these areas protects us from bad luck in the future.

Yet, the Buddha advised that living a harmless life is not enough to free ourselves. We should be pro-active in doing good things to build our merit.

The field of merit

Now I would like to look a little closer at how we generate our good fortune. As we have seen, Buddhist doctrine teaches that our good or bad fortune is set in motion by our own good or bad actions. But remember, in our World Equilibrium, the world responds in relation to the *changes* that are made upon it. It is not the amount of *good*, per se, that is returned to us, it is the amount of *change*. The amount of world response depends on how much what we have done affects the world. For example, if while driving we accidentally strike and kill a vagrant, drug-addicted thief, the world will respond in a relatively minor way. However, if we accidentally strike and kill a beloved world leader, the response of the world will be much, much larger.

Consider the following example: Let's imagine that I am a layman and I live in a house with a neighbor beside me. Suppose I hate my neighbor and stand by the fence between our yards and call him a liar and a bad guy. What would happen? Well, it's likely that the neighbor would not take too kindly to my harsh words, and would demand to know why I say such things, or perhaps call me a bad guy and a liar too.

But imagine I am not yet satisfied, so I set up a loudspeaker system and blast my accusations at full volume for the entire neighborhood to hear. What would happen this time? I think it's safe to say that the neighbor (not to mention the whole neighborhood) would be much more upset, and would probably call the police, or physically assault me himself!

In the first situation my bad action was small and the response was small. In the second both my bad action and the response were amplified. A similar effect happens with our good actions leading to a good response from the world. If we amplify our good actions, the good results are likewise amplified. For good actions the amplification system is what is termed the "Field of Merit."

The receiver amplifies the gift

In Thailand, many people take a proactive approach toward luck by consciously doing good things (making merit), thereby increasing the likelihood of good luck. It is normal for Thais to make merit before an important exam, job interview, or when trouble threatens. One way of making merit is to go to the local market where live fish are sold, and to buy a fish destined for a dinner table and release it back into the river. Another way is to donate money to a temple. But the most common form of making merit is to offer food to monks when they make their early morning alms round.

According to Buddhist doctrine the amount of merit that is received (in World Equilibrium terms) from offering alms depends on the level of the person that one makes merit with.

Different 'monks' different merit

To illustrate, imagine a Thai person making merit by offering food to seven different people dressed as monks:

The first person, though wearing a monk's robe, is actually not a monk at all, but an immoral mafia-type guy, hiding from his enemies, pretending to be a monk. He does not keep the precepts and actively engages in bad action. In this case, little good is done to the world from the food that the Thai person gave him, so let's say that the Thai person receives a single unit of merit. One unit of food given yields one unit of merit. Let's call this level 1. [Note: The extremely important factor of the intention of the giver will be examined in the second part of the book, Mind Equilibrium. Here we're focusing on *the direct, physical effect* the giving will have on the environment of the giver. The giver's World Equilibrium.]

The second person is also not a real monk, just a guy too lazy to work, who wears the orange robes so he'll get free food and a place to sleep. This guy doesn't keep the precepts, but generally is not engaged in bad actions. In this case the Thai person receives more merit – much more – on the order of one hundred times more. Let's call this level 100.

The next monk is actually a practicing monk who diligently keeps the precepts. That is, the monk lives and acts in such a way as to never intentionally cause harm to himself or other living beings. The Thai person's merit increases by another factor of 100. The goodness of the recipient amplifies the merit returning to the giver by 10,000.

The fourth monk is the real deal. He is absolutely locked in the observance of the precepts. He's not a perfect guy, but he is locked on the path.

For the rest of his life he will never intentionally break the precepts. His faith in his path is absolute and he is actively trying to do good and advance in wisdom. This type of person, whether a monk or a lay person, is known as a Stream -winner (*Sotāpanna*). The Stream-winner amplifies our Thai person's merit another 100 times. Level 1,000,000.

The fifth monk is even higher. He is endowed with all the virtues of the Stream-winner, plus, his defilements of greed, hatred, and delusion have, through practice, been reduced to a much lower level. Buddhism identifies the three defilements of greed hatred and delusion as impurities in the mind, obscuring the full awareness of reality as it is. This type of person, whether a monk or a lay person, who has reduced his defilements, is called a Once Returner (*Sakidāgāmi*), and the level is now 100,000,000.

The sixth monk is on the threshold of enlightenment. This type of person, whether a monk or a lay person, known as a Non-Returner (*Anāgāmi*), has totally eliminated greed and hatred from his mind, and has further reduced delusion. We're now at ten billion.

Our final monk is truly enlightened, an Arahant, and the level is now a staggering one trillion. Our Thai friend is fortunate indeed to make merit with an Arahant for his one unit of merit offered has been amplified a trillion times. This is the reasoning behind the one-portion-of-food-equals-many-comfortable-lives concept that I mentioned at the beginning of the book.

Comparison of Field of Merit in World Equilibrium

One unit of merit offered to:	Result in Merit Gained
Immoral person	1
Worldly person	100
Worldly person with precepts	10,000
The Stream-Winner (*Sotāpanna*)	1,000,000
The Once Returner (*Sakidāgāmī*)	100,000,000
The Non-Returner (*Anāgāmī*)	10,000,000,000
Enlightened person (*Arahanta*)	1,000,000,000,000

This may all seem quite incredible to people in this modern age, yet there is an undeniable logic to it. Wouldn't you rather help the good people so they can do more good, than help the bad so they can do more bad?

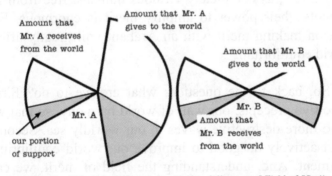

Result of Merit is different due to the difference of Field of Merit

Let us make a comparison between Mr. A and Mr. B. Their consumption of things in the world is similar. Mr. A is a good person and he is beneficial to the world. Consequently, the amount that he gives to the world is large.

On the other hand, Mr. B is a person who just lives in the world without much thought or consideration. His behavior is not stable; sometimes he is doing good and other times doing bad. The amount of good he does is much less than Mr. A.

If we have a chance to support one of them, wouldn't we choose Mr. A? Wouldn't Mr. A amplify our support, creating more good in the world? Or in more general terms, isn't it reasonable that supporting good people amplifies the amount of good given?

An Arahant is an enlightened being full of wisdom and compassion, totally free from greed, hatred and delusion – a living example of a perfected human. Such a person, has, through their own efforts, changed their own behavior until it is entirely wholesome. They have successfully completed their own self-development. Their work on themselves is finished. The remainder of their life effort is spent in service.

And so, as completely virtuous humans, free from all defilements, their power to amplify merit is enormous. For this reason making merit with an Arahant will greatly affect our world equilibrium.

So, back to the question: what are we to do? First, keep the five precepts, our wall of world harmony, so that we make no more destructive waves in our worldly sea. Second, we must actively do good to improve our world equilibrium environment. And, understanding the field of merit, we can amplify the good we do by supporting the truly good people around us.

But what about our past bad deeds that are already set in motion? Is there nothing to be done about them?

There is.

Raising ourselves above the waves

Suppose that, when I was a schoolboy, before I became a monk, I was an unfair bully to a smaller boy. I would tease and hit him, mock him and make him suffer. And now, years later, I have become a monk, and I observe all the precepts of a monk (The Buddha laid out 227 precepts that a monk must observe. For lay people, involved with family, money and worldly affairs, five precepts is enough.). Suppose now that the smaller boy had grown much larger, and he still carried a grudge. Then, in the present situation we meet, he sees that I am no longer the bullying child, but a practicing monk. I greet him and apologize for my past behavior. He will not pay me back with a punch in the mouth. Striking a good monk for his behavior as a child would be inappropriate. I have risen above the level of my childish deeds, I will never repeat them, and the effect of those childish deeds is greatly reduced.

Now suppose the same schoolboy situation, but I did not become a monk. I went on bullying. Then my former victim (grown larger and stronger and still holding a grudge) comes across me as I am bullying some new victim. I see him and disingenuously apologize for my past behavior – the former victim is much larger now.

It is very likely that I would receive my punch in the mouth. Few would shed tears for me. Striking an adult bully for his childhood bullying seems rather justified. I have remained at the level of my childish deeds and they come back to me with full force, and most likely a bit of interest.

Let's go back to the mass murderer who became enlightened, Angulimala, remember him? He murdered over a thousand people on his teacher's instruction. Suppose the king had found him before the Buddha did. He would have been punished as the murderer that he was. I'm sure they had many ways to punish people then, and he would have received the worst. Few would question him receiving the harshest of punishments.

But the Buddha found him first and Angulimala became one of the luckiest people in history. But luck of course, is a matter of our own past deeds returning...

Angulimala did his murderous deeds as a man without precepts – a man of a value of one. If he remained at that low level, the action of his deeds would have returned to him, from the same level, like a tsunami. Yet he didn't remain at that level. With the help of the Buddha, he broke through his delusional fog and saw a higher truth which he took to heart. He went from a murderer to a truly moral man who wouldn't hurt a fly. It reminds me of the story behind the song Amazing Grace. A slave trader sees the Light. In Buddhist terms though we would say that his own value increased, made him high and stable, and the tsunami hit, but didn't wash him away.

It just hit him in the head with sticks and stones. He had a giant wave of karma coming for him, but by the time it arrived he had become an even larger giant. Mathematically it looks like this:

$$\frac{\text{Karma}}{1} \longrightarrow \frac{\text{Karma}}{1 \text{ trillion}}$$

So let's suppose that in the past we kept no precepts – nothing was beneath us: lying, stealing, and even raping and killing. Huge, violent, killer waves, of our own making, are bearing down on us, ready to smash us against the rocks. Then somehow, we see more clearly, we improve ourselves, we reject our past behavior and we embrace the five precepts. Our value has increased ten thousand times. Or put another way, the power of our bad deeds to affect us has been reduced ten thousand times. The waves will hit us, we can't stop them, but they only take a limb or an eye or some teeth. We are left alive. The five precepts will reduce the negative effects from our past.

Furthermore when we are living on the higher moral ground of the five precepts, we are operating in a cleaner, more moral, more benevolent environment. We are surrounded by more good. Smooth harmonious action is more the norm. In addition, people are attracted to others at the same moral level, so as you improve yourself you will find yourself in the company of more moral people. This new, higher network is a valuable asset. You can find good friends, good customers, and even a good partner for your life. Thus in this higher moral environment it's easier to reach your goals and realize your dreams. It's easier to receive good, because you're in a good place. And more help is available because you're surrounded by good people. This is also the power of the precepts.

And it's not all or nothing. Suppose you can only keep four precepts, but can't break away from the alcohol or drugs. You get some measure of protection for keeping the four. A lot better than nothing. So keep as many precepts as you can. It will help you build power until you can keep all five, steady as a rock.

But remember, the precepts must be held with intention. You must actively uphold them, reminding yourself throughout the day that you are a person who doesn't kill, who doesn't take what is not given, who doesn't engage in sexual misconduct, who doesn't lie, and who doesn't take drugs or alcohol. It's the conscious, active holding of these virtues, that give them their power.

There is another old story in Buddhism about an enlightened disciple of the Buddha, who was beset upon, again and again, by a group of robbers who wanted to beat him to death. With his Arahant mindfulness and power he was able to continually avoid their clutches. He thus avoided his attackers accruing the karma of having killed an Arahant. However, in the end, he saw that it was time, and he submitted himself to them, allowing them to smash his body to death, breaking every bone in his body. So even as an Arahant it's possible to have old karma strong enough to have one's life violently taken.

For most of us our past karma is not so strong. Yet, when we make merit to improve our world equilibrium and offset the effects of past bad actions, we should be mindful of the type of merit we make.

We can think of merit like medicine – each medicine is specific for a type of disease. If I have stolen money, or have a problem with money, my merit-making should involve money. If I have been untruthful, or have a problem with truthfulness, my merit-making should involve truthfulness.

To be most effective the medicine must match the disease. Yet, what if I have taken a person's life? What can be done then? Maybe it's best to leave that question as food for thought.

A tale of two arrows and a hot-head

To review some of these concepts, imagine one hypothetical morning in our chain of lifetimes. In this hypothetical lifetime we are a worldly person, not too bad, but not especially good either – sometimes we can be a bit hot-headed. On this particular morning, unbeknownst to us, two karmic arrows, feedback from our past action, are coming towards us. The first is a small arrow of good karma. The second a big, powerful, dangerous arrow of bad karma. We made and launched them both at some point in our past. For whatever reason, conditions are such that they both arrive today.

The first good-karma arrow arrives as we are at home preparing to go to work. We look in the mirror, and get the feeling that today something weird may happen, maybe something bad. At the same time we also remember that the five precepts are a kind of protection from the bad. We want that protection. So we decide that today we will be a real five-precepts person. We connect with what we hold sacred and lock our intention on keeping the precepts. At that moment our level in the field of merit increases one hundred times.

We leave the house feeling different than normal, more alert, because today we are a five-precepts person.

As we're driving to work, the highway traffic is heavy but still moving fast – the way we like it. One of our habitual pet-peeves is bad drivers, especially drivers who cut us off on the highway. Our usual reaction to being cut off is to hit the horn and aggressively tailgate the perpetrator. Today we remind ourselves that we are keeping the five precepts. Today we are better than our bad habits.

That very second the bad arrow arrives. Suddenly some reckless driver swerves into our lane without warning. Our cool head, from keeping the precepts, holds us back from our habitual response, and instead of hitting the horn and tailgating, we take a deep breath and back off on our speed. The reckless driver swerves again, clips the guardrail and flips, right in front of us, like some Hollywood action movie. But instead of being right behind him, we're far enough back to react a little, hit the brakes and turn away from the most deadly impact.

Our car is wrecked, and we find ourselves in the hospital with a few fractured ribs. On a normal day we would have been killed. But because we were keeping the precepts, our bad karma had one hundred times less destructive force in our world.

We could not stop the bad-karma arrow, after all we made it our self; we sent it to our self; but we could change the self to which it arrives. We made our self a higher-level person, so the bad arrow had lost most of its energy by the time it got to us. And remember too, we were keeping the precepts because we felt the first arrow of good karma, and heeded its warning. Small arrows of good karma can be wonderful things. After all, they are gifts we made and sent to ourselves.

Ultimately, we cannot know, in any full sense, the details of our old karma. Buddhist teaching considers it a waste of time to dwell on what we may or may not have been or done in our past lives. It's past and done. Let it go. Better to focus on the principles at work. This moment now is much more important.

> Our intention and our commitment
> not to harm ourselves or others
> diminishes the impact
> of our returning bad karma.

A wise person acts on this knowledge.

Ten Wholesome Actions

At this point it might be of value to clarify what we mean by "doing good." Buddhism identifies ten wholesome courses of action *(Ten Kusala)* – four verbal, three bodily, and three mental. This goes beyond the five precepts in spelling out actions that are considered moral, correct and wholesome. The mental actions directly affect our Mental Equilibrium and both bodily and verbal actions directly affect our World Equilibrium.

Wholesome Bodily Actions
1. Avoid killing; act in a way that cares for, respects and supports life. (precept one)
2. Avoid taking what is not given; act in a way that respects others' property. (precept two)
3. Avoid sexual misconduct; act in a way that respects others and respects society's sexual morals. (precept three)

Wholesome Verbal Actions
4. Avoid lying – especially for the sake of advantage. (precept four)
5. Avoid malicious speech; speak to unite those in discord, to encourage, and to make harmony.
6. Avoid harsh language; speak gentle, loving, courteous and agreeable words.
7. Avoid frivolous talk; speak at the right time in accordance with facts, what is useful, moderate, and full of sense.

Wholesome Mental Actions
8. Be free from covetousness and craving.
9. Be free from ill will; hope for the best for all beings.
10. Accept as fact that there are results from both wholesome and unwholesome acts.

Mental Equilibrium

Now that we have discussed protecting ourselves and maintaining a benevolent equilibrium with our external world, I would like to discuss our internal world. This is the world of our true power source, our intention. Here we are going to talk about the heart of karma: our intentions and our perceptions, our use of our free will and the framework in which all this occurs.

Again we can use the metaphor of floating in a pool of water. This time the pool represents our mental world. Every thought/intention we have sends out waves into this pool. All of these waves taken together, along with echoes of our old waves, form our mental environment. If we fill our mental environment with angry waves, then that is where our mind lives, seeing angry waves everywhere. Similarly, if we use our mind wisely and compassionately, we will find our pool becoming clearer and more beautiful. The vista we see will be something to behold. Our mental environment is up to us.

Our world equilibrium is actually a relatively minor issue when compared with our mental equilibrium. The state of our world equilibrium makes us more or less comfortable as we live out our lives, but it is our mental activity, our volition, perception and intention, the way we *use* our mind, that paints our world; the way we use our mind literally creates our heavens and hells, and issues us the tickets to journey there.

Let's go back to our previous illustration:

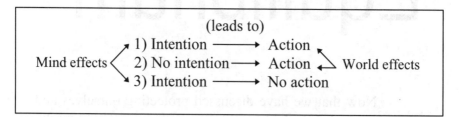

We have two occasions of intention – with and without action. When intention leads to action the world is affected, and when intention does not lead to action the world is not affected. Yet on both occasions the mind is affected by its own processes.

Our mind affects itself. Every thought in our mind creates new mental conditions. Each new mental condition feeds back into the process of creating new thoughts. Thus our mind is creating while simultaneously receiving feedback from its own previous creation.

The processing mind

The mind is a truly miraculous processor. Every moment that our mind exists within this body it perceives different categories of things through the different physical sensory organs: it sees forms with the eyes, hears sounds with the ears, smells smells with the nose, tastes tastes with the tongue, and feels the touch and pull of the world by bodily contact.

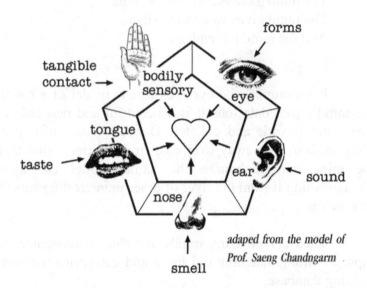

adaped from the model of
Prof. Saeng Chandngarm

Through these five sensory gates we have all come to know beauty, ugliness, color, light, and darkness; the sound of footsteps and our mother's voice; silence, speech and melody; the smell of smoke, farts, rotting carcasses, fresh-baked bread and flowers; the taste of milk, chilis, and bile; the bite of a cold wind, the heat of the sun, and the warmth of a hand; the softness of a baby's cheek and the roughness of a cat's tongue; the lightness of a feather, and the weight of our own body.

This is all the mind's data. This is how our mind touches our environment. Through these different sensory gates the mind contacts the world.

The mind gathers and collates data.
The mind gives value to the data.
And the mind remembers.

For example, the eye sees a new model of a car that the mind's past data tells it is a beautiful and desirable car. The mind records and collates. One day later, with just a glimpse from a freeway overpass, from a brief visual input, the mind can recognize the same model car again, distinguishing it from the river of other uninteresting cars that pass below.

Thus our amazing minds are able to recognize new input as fitting/matching old input and categories within the existing database.

Let's use the word perception for this process of reaching back to old data to compare and match with new input. Perception is the process of using previous memories/ data-input (involving one or more sensory organs) as criteria for deciding whether some new input is interesting or boring, good or bad, whether it will bring happiness or suffering.

The creating mind

The process of perception itself can also be recorded as new data. This new data is then sorted and categorized into the database. The model car we glimpse from the overpass is exiting the freeway towards a wealthy neighborhood. Our mind imagines ourselves driving that car and we imagine the feel of the leather seats and the tightness of the steering and the new-car smell and the quiet coolness of the expensive interior. We imagine ourselves pulling into the perfect driveway of our perfect house for an evening of leisure and joy. All this data – mental data – is also recorded and sorted. These are objects that come to the mind, from the mind. These mental perceptions are the result of our thinking, reprocessing, imagining, pondering, and concocting. We Thai people love our food, so I call this process *mental cooking*. There are many ways to cook. But we should cook well, with good, pure ingredients, because our mind eats everything we cook.

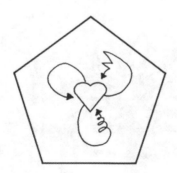

The deciding mind

How does the mind make a decision? According to Buddhist doctrine, the mind uses whatever is remembered, whatever has been decided, valued, or qualified in the past as the basis for making a new decision.

It goes like this: The eye sees that new car. From the past data input (both external and mental cooking) the mind remembers that this is a car, a car that I like, a car that I want, a car of high status, a car that will make me happy. The mind quickly decides – good picture, good car. This subliminally fast action is the act of perception. Similarly the ear hears the rattle and clunk that my present car makes. From the past data input (both external and mental cooking) the mind remembers that this is the sound of wearing out, aging, breaking down, of low status. The mind quickly decides, bad sound, and quite possibly, bad car. All of this data, the form (the sight and sound) and the judgment (good and bad), are kept as new data in the mind.

And so it goes, thought after thought.

The digital mind

The Buddhist teachings say that the activity of the mind is digital, not analog. The mind processes information in discrete units. Each unit has three phases: arising, existing and ceasing.

The arising, existing and ceasing of the mind occurs at a very high frequency. The Buddhist teachings from 2500 years ago stated that in the time it takes to snap your fingers, the mind cycles one trillion times. So if we assume that it takes a quarter second to snap your fingers, we have a frequency in the ballpark of 4 trillion (that's a 4 with 12 zeros) cycles per second. Thus, to us, our mind appears smooth and continuous, much as the flickering light from a fluorescent bulb, or the images on a movie screen appear like a steady stream. The Buddhist teachings say the mind is not a smooth continuum; the mind arises, exists, and ceases – very, very quickly.

As long as we are alive in this body the mind will be active at some level, arising at the moment of perception, existing, ceasing, arising again. Sometimes the mind perceives new data from an external source, other times it takes its own activity as the thing that it perceives, following itself along the links of its own chain. Other times, such as deep sleep, the mind is quiet, and moments come and go without perception. Yet on an even deeper level, below our perception, the mind is still active. All of these moments are recorded.

The new moments come on top of the old ones. Layer after layer. In the dimension of mind, space is not a problem – there is room for all memories. Despite what overworked students may say, the mind is never full. The mental fatigue students sometimes feel is due to lack of mental power. The power of perception may be limited by ability, lack of training or lack of exercise, but consciousness itself is unlimited.

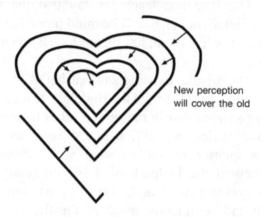

New perception
will cover the old

You've probably read reports or seen movies where a person who couldn't consciously recall anything of value about some important event that they witnessed was hypnotized to help them remember. Then, in that different state of consciousness they were able to remember details that their conscious mind never even registered in the first place.

Now, I know, there are many times in the real world, where people think they remember something, but in fact it is merely an expression of something else in their mind or feelings. Of course. Nature works like that too. That said, Buddhist teaching says that all that mind touches is recorded. Anything that travels through the gates of our physical sensory organs to reach our mind is recorded. Wow.

The memory of a Buddha

On a full moon night in May, more that 2500 years ago, sitting under a Bo tree, a man, a former prince, named Gotama Sakya, attained enlightenment. His enlightenment was the fruit of countless lives of striving to know the truth of existence. These lifetimes of personal effort had built up in him a truly massive reserve of power. So much so, that on that night, when his mundane human vision unclouded, he saw before him all his past lives. He saw how the laws of nature had acted through the eons of his own life-stream, and he came to truly know and understand the workings of karma. But where did these ancient memories come from? They came from the data bank of his own mind.

From our entrance into this physical cycle of existence eons ago, up to this very moment, our minds have been recording. All events, in all the processes of our life are stored. Yet accessing this information is problematic. If I ask you where you were last Sunday at three in the afternoon, you may not be able to answer confidently. This is because, in the minds of ordinary people, newer events come and overlay on top of the older events, covering them, causing them to be forgotten. Furthermore, in the minds of most of us, our data is often somewhat jumbled and disorganized. Some data encourage one action, other data discourage it, or encourage the opposite. The mind of a Buddha is much more organized.

The Buddha's long training involved aligning all the data of his mind towards a single consistent goal: the proper understanding of reality as it is – enlightenment. This involved lifetime after lifetime focused on that single goal. Finally, once critical mass of properly aligned knowledge was reached, the Buddha attained enlightenment.

All Bodhisattvas (those who strive to become Buddhas: find the truth of nature by their own power and bring this truth to the world) must prepare this critical mass of aligned knowledge – all of it directed toward their goal of enlightenment. And so, as a Bodhisattva, the Buddha's training was so immense that the power of his mind was great enough to access his full mental data base. He could look back on all of his past lives, seeing how intention, action and karma had acted. Normal people who haven't practiced lifetime after lifetime don't have that kind of ability. Not by a long shot.

But we can benefit from the insight that he gained from seeing how karma had acted throughout his chain of lifetimes. He saw the cause of suffering in intricate detail. And he saw the end of suffering; an attainable goal for all.

After his enlightenment the Buddha spent more than forty years teaching others so that they could understand enough to permanently free themselves from suffering. The teaching is self-consistent, logical and does not require a leap of faith. Untold thousands have followed his teachings and reached total freedom; and there are enlightened people on the planet right now.

the process of mind

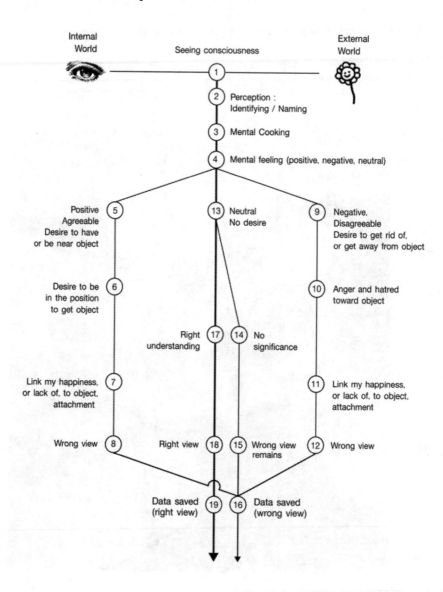

Internal World — Seeing consciousness — External World

1

2 Perception : Identifying / Naming

3 Mental Cooking

4 Mental feeling (positive, negative, neutral)

Positive 5 Agreeable Desire to have or be near object

13 Neutral No desire

9 Negative, Disagreeable Desire to get rid of, or get away from object

Desire to be 6 in the position to get object

10 Anger and hatred toward object

Right 17 understanding

14 No significance

Link my happiness, 7 or lack of, to object, attachment

11 Link my happiness, or lack of, to object, attachment

Wrong view 8

Right view 18

15 Wrong view remains

12 Wrong view

Data saved 19 (right view)

16 Data saved (wrong view)

The process of mind – a closer look

Let's take a closer look at the process of perception. Let's imagine an ordinary situation, when we are in a normal state of awareness, in our everyday reality, and we see some normal object. Let's use the diagram on the opposite page to follow the process.

The first steps

1) My internal sense organ, my eye in this case, and an external object make contact. There is seeing. This is an instantaneous contact prior to any thinking. Light, photons, reflection, retina, optic nerve. Buddhism refers to this as a kind of consciousness – an awareness of an object.

2) Next, the object is compared to my memory data base and identified; the object is named: it is a car, a bird, a person.... With this identification comes a quality, also retrieved from my memory data banks, which is attached to the object: good, delightful, fashionable, ugly, boring, or beautiful.

3) Quick bursts of mental activities then arise around the object and its quality (mental cooking). Buddhist teaching calls this a another kind of consciousness – the mental formations that occur using our old data, the new image and our present intention. Our intention may be wholesome or unwholesome, or a mix of both. Here, in this flash of mental activity, we are creating our karma.

4) A mental feeling arises as a result of the previous mental activities concerning the object. My intention/cooking (cause) creates a mental feeling (result). Cause and effect. From this point forward in the flowchart, I am experiencing the results of my own intention. The mental feeling may be agreeable, disagreeable, or neutral.

The positive branch

5) If the mental feeling is agreeable it will cause a desire to have or be near the object.

6) The desire to acquire or be near the object creates another desire: the desire to be in a position to obtain access to the object. For example, I see a luxury car; it is agreeable to me. I desire to have it. I desire to be rich enough to get it. The Buddhists call this second desire the desire to be. It is the desire to be in the position to get the thing that you want.

7) This will lead to the formation of a link or bond between me and the object. That object is seen as a way to obtain happiness. I think that if I have that object, then I will be happy. Buddhists call this step attachment.

8) At this point, a mere fraction of a second after seeing the object, I now believe that this object can help me obtain happiness. Buddhist teaching explains clearly that no object can bring any kind of lasting happiness. Objects come and objects go. If I seek happiness in objects (be they cars, birds or people) then I misunderstand the nature of objects. I have what Buddhists call wrong view.

The negative branch

9) If the mental feeling is disagreeable it will cause a desire to get away from the object, a desire to get rid of it.

10) This desire to be rid of the object creates an unsatisfactory feeling, a feeling of anger or hatred toward that object. That object is an obstacle, a fly in my ointment. (However slight it may be, Buddhist teaching says that the desire to be rid of something always contains a portion of hatred. Always.) For example, I see a car blocking my way in a traffic jam. I desire to be rid of this traffic jam and free to move on towards my home. I have an aversion, and hatred for traffic jams, anger towards the bumper in front of me.

11) This aversion leads to the formation of a link or bond between me and the object. That object is seen as an obstruction to my happiness. I think that if that thing is there, I cannot be happy. Buddhists call this step attachment.

12) At this point, a mere fraction of a second after seeing the object, I now believe that this object can prevent me from obtaining happiness. Buddhist teaching clearly explains that objects cannot block happiness. Objects come and objects go. If I think that happiness is not possible in the presence of some objects, then I misunderstand the nature of objects. I have what Buddhists call wrong view.

The neutral branch

13) If the mental feeling is neutral, there is no desire associated with the object. This is the proper mental disposition according to Buddhism. However, this neutrality could have two causes.

14) One cause is that the thing has no significance for me. I'm not interested in it, so I don't generate positive or negative mental feelings, but my lack of interest is not due to wisdom.

15) My wrong view concerning the object remains, but there is no desire associated with the object, so I let it go. I create no karma, yet I remain in my ignorance. Should this object later obtain significance or importance, I will choose to desire or be rid of it. But for now, I just don't care.

Data saved

16) All of this data – positive, negative, insignificant – is saved. Yet all is flawed. The glass is still dark. I remain in ignorance and do not see objects for what they are. My mind is not seeing reality as it really is. I am not seeing the truth of nature. Instead I am seeing an artificial value that I have added myself. I falsely see external sense objects as able to bring or prevent happiness. This means that my next conscious moment arises from a base of wrong view, a base of ignorance.

The middle way

17) There is another pathway on the neutral branch – the only path that avoids wrong view. The branch of understanding and wisdom. On this path, objects that I once strongly desired appear to me now as mere eye-candy. Objects that once made me angry are like spilled milk. I have come to understand these objects for what they truly are. They no longer cause me to desire or to hate.

18) I see the true nature of these objects; objects come and objects go; they have no connection to my happiness or sorrow, so they have no power over me. This is called right view. This is the path of wisdom. This is the path of Buddhism.

19) This data is recorded and saved. Thus we begin our next conscious moment from a base of right view. What this book, and the Buddhist teaching, is trying to do is to help us to follow the path of right understanding. Seeing nature as it is. [The interested reader will benefit from studying The Three Characteristics, The Four Noble Truths, and The Law of Dependent Origination. These teachings are briefly outlined in the back of the book.]

So to summarize: Nature is constantly changing, objects come and objects go. So we should train our minds to see and acknowledge that fact. It's foolish and unskillful to cling to something which will change, breakdown, and cease to be. We should understand that our attachment leads to unsatisfactory feelings and then strive to rid ourselves of our attachments.

And what is the source of our attachment? It comes from the false value that we added to the object. And where does the false value come from? From our wrong view of nature, our ignorance, our failure to see reality as it is. Ignorance is the first link in the chain leading to our suffering.

Integrated habits – our mental baseline

If you remember, in our World Equilibrium we said that our action and intention go out into the world, disturbing it, eventually to return to us, perhaps in this life, perhaps in another future life. Well, Mental Equilibrium is a little different. Our intentions and perceptions in our mental environment, over time, tend to create a kind of baseline mental state. The more recent intentions have a stronger effect on this state than our older data, yet all our mental data contribute to our baseline. From this baseline we view the world, process data, and do our mental cooking. Different baselines will lead us to cook our new input in different ways. And remember, we eat all we cook.

For example, imagine two men who see the same beautiful young woman walk past. One man experiences joy at seeing her beauty. He notices the dignified poise of her motion, the freshness of youth in her face and the joy and intelligence in her eyes. He smiles and silently wishes her well. The second man sees only her outer form. He experiences a surge of lust and imagines having sex with her. These two men are operating from different baselines. These baselines were built up layer by layer, moment by moment from their own intention and mental processes.

So we are all responsible for our own mental environment. If it is dirty or rusty or dull it is only ourselves who can clean it up and make it shine. In one of the Buddha's most famous sermons he simplified his teachings into three simple, straightforward admonitions:

Stop doing bad things.

Do more good things.

Purify your mind.

We are mind

Our moment by moment reality is the reality of our mind. Our mental world is where we live, the place we cannot leave, where all our experiences exist. If I put my hand in a fire it is my mind, not my hand, that experiences the pain. Had the nerve impulses been blocked I wouldn't have felt a thing. But in our natural condition, with nerve impulses free to flow, the feedback from our body screams pain at our mind. In that burning instant my mind is in hell, my mind's connection to the physical is a connection to pain and agony. Though, it should be noted, with training, one is able to greatly reduce even physical pain by controlling the action of one's mind.

In our dreams at night we can feel pleasure, fear, anxiety, boredom or joy or any of the vast array of feelings we experience while awake. As we dream, we exist in the reality of our dream. It is at that moment for us, true. Our pulse quickens or slows, we sweat, twitch or moan. Yet around our body as we sleep in bed, all is quiet. Our mind is on a journey someplace while our physical body remains in bed, and to our mind it is real.

Buddhism suggests that if we look carefully, we will see that the thing we call 'me' is our mind.

The creative human,
membrane between heaven and hell

While we have a life as a human, our mind works through the physical brain and human form, using it as a transducer between the mental and physical worlds. This productive connection between the human brain and the mind is the reason behind the great power and importance that Buddhism puts on being born human. Only as a human do we have this wonderful power to put our intention into the physical world. As a human we can exercise our free will and stamp it on physical reality. As an animal, while we still have feeling and emotion, our free will and intention are so small as to be negligible when compared to the human. As an angel, while enjoying bliss and beauty, we are more or less disconnected from the physical world.

In total, the Buddhist teachings speak of 31 different realms of existence from lowest hell to highest heaven, all of which are subject to the laws of birth and decay, all of which are on the wheel of life and death. Humanity is poised at the key position, the balance point, like a membrane between the higher and the lower. At this position our mind/brain transducer projects all our imbalanced intentions and actions up and down through all levels of creation. Our divine intentions are projected into the heavenly zones and our hellish intention projected into the hellish zones. These echoes of intention create structures and forms at the levels corresponding to the quality of the associated intention.

Our human intention is creative. Moment by moment, human lifetime after human lifetime our imbalanced intentions build for ourselves divine and hellish structures. We build ourselves heaven and we build ourselves hell. They are both quite real, and they are both the creations of our mind.

In this way, the hell to which a Thai person may go, may be quite different from the hell of an African, European, or international traveler. Our different mental conditions built different structures. The suffering and woe are the same but the implements and settings appear different. Likewise our heavens may appear different, but the bliss and joy are the same. And each structure has been created by the occupant over the course of their many human lives.

So, according to the Buddhist teachings, the human is the most creative of all possible forms of existence. As humans we create as we please, and our creation resonates through all levels of existence. We are both responsible for, and subject to, our own creation. We cannot turn off this creative power. Whether we are mindful or not, we are creating at every moment. Through this mind-to-human-form transducer we create our own joys and our own sadness, our own prisons, or ultimately our own freedom.

Being born a human is a truly fantastic opportunity! We have tremendous creative power! Don't waste it. Human bodies are not always available. In the four or five billion years that the earth has been around, humans have only been here for at best a few hundred thousand years. We are all immensely fortunate to be here, now, in human form. Let's make the best of this marvelous opportunity. This is our chance. Let's take it.

I wish you well, my friend.

The layered mind, bodily death and rebirth

Every time our mind perceives an object through our sense-bases, an intention arises. This intention can be thought of as a kind of mind-stuff, a building block of the mental environment. Each perception/intention unit covers the previous one, layer by layer. Even this very moment, as you read these words, layers of intention are being laid down in rapid succession with the speed of mind.

> By coming to understand the law of nature, the action of karma, and the truth about the cause of our suffering, we will gain the ability to maintain a proper disposition towards this world around us. Keeping the Five Precepts will become second nature and our layers of data, built up moment by moment, will become cleaner and clearer. We will be very glad to have such a good data base when our body dies.

At the time of bodily death our internal collection of mind-stuff takes on new importance, because as the physical senses shut down, our connection with the physical world is broken, and we are left with only our mental objects. Disconnected from the stream of input from the bodily senses, the mind becomes aware that the body is going to die, and, shaken and frightened, the mind looks for some input, for something to grasp. It is similar to a person who has suddenly lost the home where they have lived their entire life. Such a person is disoriented, and will quickly look for another place to stay, contacting friends or family or anyone who can help.

And, as the mind is unable to find assistance through the physical senses, it turns back to data already perceived and stored. This is very much like one's life flashing before one's eyes; and remember, the mind is very fast.

The key issue is: as the images flash by, what past data point of consciousness does the mind grasp as it disconnects from the body?

This final moment of perception is important because the qualities and characteristics of that final unit of perception will condition the new form that the mind takes. It will condition the next rebirth. Yet for the untrained mind, the data flashes by much too quickly for the mind to consciously choose. It's something like musical chairs; when the music stops you grab the nearest chair.

In the unfortunate case of a person who has lived a selfish, reckless life and committed some truly terrible act – for example, matricide – then, this powerful negative data point, extremely out of balance with nature, will rise like great flash and attract the mind. There will be almost no way to avoid this mental data; the mind will be inescapably drawn to it, and the subsequent rebirth will be adversely conditioned.

Luckily, few of us have such extreme karmic acts to rebalance. For those of us with more normal karma, yet still untrained in controlling our minds, it is quite likely that we will end up with a data point from the data bank of our own habitual action. It's simply statistics. We have more habitual data than anything else. This habitual data could be good or bad.

For example if someone worked in a slaughterhouse killing animals every day, a lot of these data points will be flashing by. It's not unlikely that the mind will end up with one of these data points when the music stops, experiencing the harmful killing intention of that moment, and possibly experience rebirth in the animal realm, the realm of fear, in order to re-assimilate the mental condition they have created.

On the positive side, a nurse or teacher may have an abundance of data points related to helping another person, relieving suffering, or passing on wisdom. With so many such data points it's not unlikely that they will end up with a thought of loving-kindness and compassion as their final unit of perception. Thus in the next thought interval following physical death, the mind expresses loving kindness and compassion. This action, as always, immediately expresses itself as a new (non-physical) body matching those mental qualities. This is angelic rebirth. Rebirth into a finer angelic body; into a heaven that has literally been built from the mind-stuff of their previous good intentions and mental actions, a personally made paradise.

While in such a heavenly state they are literally consuming their good karma. Finally, as their heavenly intention bank account decreases, they will reach a point where they can no longer stay where they are. The heavenly intention of their death-data point has run its course and expired. The next previous data point is then retrieved from the data stack, to act as the template for the next rebirth. And so it goes.

In Thailand it is normal to remind our loved ones, as they are dying, of meritorious actions that they have done in the past. Reminding a dying grandmother, for example, of how she gave food to young monks at sunrise, morning after morning. It is a happy memory for the grandmother. Her mind is filled with loving kindness, generosity and joy, and so, as her mind detaches from her body, it immediately expresses itself as a new (non-physical) body corresponding to those positive states. Pleasant final thoughts lead to pleasant rebirths.

Rebirth and movie tickets

Bodily death is a transition from one type of mental housing to another. The last thought/intention that we have as we leave our human house will condition the next 'housing' we acquire – and equally important – the next neighborhood. I like to think of this final thought at the threshold, as a ticket to our next movie. But remember, the speed of mind is very fast, so our tickets are being created very quickly. If our thought is about goodness and joy then our ticket will take us to see a movie of goodness and joy. The duration of the movie depends on the duration and intensity of the intention behind the thought – the number of tickets we made. A strong, intense, sustained thought of good will, gives us a whole series of tickets, allowing us to step into a long, good movie.

Furthermore, Buddhist literature indicates that the time frame of angelic or hellish realms is different from ours. A few moments here can be a long, long time in either heaven or hell. Each ticket, created in a flash, corresponds to a much longer duration in heaven or hell.

Let's imagine a hypothetical moment of death. Let's assume that we are basically a good person, not locked in the five precepts, but averaging toward the good. We are driving our car on the highway, thinking nice thoughts of our family as usual. Suddenly a careless driver cuts us off and forces us off the road. We have a flash of animal rage at the driver's reckless incompetence, and we try to regain control of our car as it heads off the road. Then straight ahead of us we see a kid on a bicycle. With compassion, we immediately think, "No way, I will not hurt that kid." We counter steer the only way that's left to us, and we smash into a light post. At that moment we die.

ticket number one:

Because of the loving-kindness and compassion that we showed for the kid on the bike during our final thought moment, we have a bunch of heavenly tickets in our hand. Thus, in the next moment, we find ourselves surrounded by goodness, angels and all the beauty of heaven.

Our last thought/intention became the scaffolding on which our next 'body' was formed. Our thought was filled with loving-kindness and compassion for a stranger. This gave us a heavenly body in heaven. A body not of flesh and blood, but a finer, angelic body, not tied so strongly to matter. We have our mind and we can experience things around us which are perfectly real to us. And because we are less attached to the physical, we are not troubled by old age or sickness. We are surrounded by heaven's beauty. We are beautiful. We feel no pain. It seems perfect, but for one thing: it cannot last.

The power of our final thought/intention brought us to heaven. Like a series of movie tickets, properly paid for, entitle us to see the corresponding film.

Depending on the duration and intensity of our threshold intention – the number and value of the tickets - this pleasant movie may last a long or short time. Either way, our time in heaven will be much, much longer than the duration of that final thought, but, the movie will end when our tickets run out. One day our heavenly friends may see us fade from view as the energy of our final thought reaches completion. We then come to the next series of tickets, our second-to-the-last human thought.

ticket number two:

In our highway death scenario, our second-to-last thought was anger at the bad driver, so we drop from heaven into one of the hellish realms. Anger takes us to a land of burning and violence and pain. Everything is real for us in our hell body and our mind suffers. But our time in hell is not a form of punishment, but the natural result of our destructive intention. It is natural law in action. Our angry intention built us a (non-physical) hell body corresponding to our mental state. We sent our self to hell. Thankfully though, this series of tickets too, will not last forever, and when the intention has been rebalanced, we will then move on to our next previous thought.

ticket number three:

Our third-to-last thought was one of our habitual thoughts: nice thoughts of our family. This is a thought that sends no harm to the world. It is a thought of a moral human, and it will lead us into the possibility of human rebirth. I say possibility because, unlike heaven and hell, humanity is connected to the physical, so some physical requirements are necessary before rebirth is possible – namely the physical ability of a woman to conceive and deliver a baby.

Past karmic connections with others may lead us to be born into families with whom we have shared past lives. Buddhism has many stories of people traveling through their lives in groups – sometimes we are the brother, sometimes the mother, sometimes the lover, sometimes the best friend.

There are also many stories of people coming into conflict again and again, in a tit for tat intertwined chain of lives. I killed you last life, and this life you kill me, and in next lives we may do it again. This ignorant cycle of violence need not continue – all we need to do is to exercise our free will to upgrade our behavior, view the world with loving-kindness and compassion, and take control of ourselves.

Our karma is a factor, at times a strong and powerful factor, but what we actually do is up to us. Up to our free will.

Now, back to our tickets. Ticket number three took us back to humanity.

If we are fortunate enough to be reborn human, then the remaining tickets in our hand join the stack of accumulated knowledge that our mind carries. And as we begin another human life, we act from this baseline of accumulated subconscious knowledge and begin generating new tickets. And so our chain of lives continues.

So to recap: Our thought/intentions at the moment of death are like tickets that direct us to various rebirths. From heaven or hell, we don't really have the power to generate new tickets, so we continue moving backwards through the tickets we generated as a human until we make it back to the human realm. Once human again, the old tickets join our massive subconscious data stack, and with our new human intention we begin generating new tickets.

For those who are curious, Buddhism says that animals have some ability to generate new tickets. This power is much less than the human, but it is sufficient to trap some in a long chain of animal rebirths. We're born a dog, for example, people feed us, we lay around, get taken on walks, and we think with our dog brain – not bad. I like it. And so we get reborn as a dog again and again. Eventually though, we will grow dissatisfied with the limitations of a dog's life and we will move on. But Buddhism warns of this animal trap, because as an animal we cannot benefit from understanding the truth of nature. As humans though, we can benefit from knowing the truth – we can develop ourselves. This is why human life is so valuable.

In a similar way heaven can be considered a trap. Buddhists regard it as a less useful and productive life than a human's life. So, beautiful as a long heavenly life is, it could be thought of as a poor use of one's time. Furthermore, the beauty and ease and comfort of heaven can spoil us and give us habits which can make our re-entry into humanity a painful one. So, for a Buddhist, heaven is not an ultimate goal, but, for a normal, untrained person, it's a much more preferable rebirth than some of the alternatives.

And speaking of re-entry, imagine now a new baby. A Buddhist would not call the baby pure and innocent and lacking experience. Neither would they call the baby guilty. Rather, they would view the baby as a consciousness reborn with latent habits and predispositions, and karmic connections with this world and with the father and mother.

Managing our relationship with our iceberg

For a while now we have been talking about rebirth and the possibility of developing ourselves. But when we mention rebirth, it is clearly not "our normal self" (whatever that is) which is reborn. After all, we usually can't remember our past lives. It is something else – a kind of subconscious knowledge or information imprint, created from our past experience and especially our past intention. This is mind. My mind. Your mind. Not the busy local mind that remembers where I left my keys – but the mind beneath that mind. The mind that makes me, me. If we imagine an iceberg, I picture the mind that is reborn as the part beneath the surface, and the mind that stores the details of this life as the part above the surface. The subsurface part of each of us contains the past wisdom that we have accumulated through our countless (and I do mean countless) lives. It also contains a lot of confused data at cross purposes.

Yet even though this vast subsurface part of us may not be directly accessible or observable to our conscious mind, it is still attached to us. It houses not only our wisdom and treasure, but also our foolishness and filth.

Our layer of ice

The *subsurface* iceberg has two distinct parts: The huge part that comes along as historic baggage from our past lives, and the part closer to the surface that we have added in this present lifetime. This part near the surface, our present-lifetime contribution, is of great interest. It is key.

This top layer is our interface with our deep subsurface mass – and all the good and bad that is there. Communication between our waking consciousness and the deep ice must pass through this upper layer. We are building this upper layer, even now, moment by moment. We can control this layer. We can make this layer, this connection zone, work for us.

Our thoughts in the present can create a buffer, or a filter, in this top layer interface zone. For example, a person who is locked in the five precepts has a powerful filter that will prevent any and all subconscious urges from arising that would lead to breaking a precept.

So while our final thoughts at the moment of death lead us into our next life/movie, *the billions of thoughts and intentions during the moments of our lives, continually form and re-form our connection to our subconscious iceberg.* And this connection moves with our iceberg through the chain of our lives. This top layer is always in place, just beneath the waves as the next moment, or the next lifetime, begins. Such is the tremendous journey of our minds.

We are all developing and gaining wisdom, in our own way, at our own pace. But the development of even the slowest of us – when viewed from the long, long, long time frame of our chain of lives – is not in question. We are evolving. You and me. Our minds are on an amazing journey of evolution.

The evolving mind

Imagine a single cell in our body, say a neuron. It is taking in nutrients, expelling waste, moving and controlling chemicals, manufacturing molecules, reading RNA messages and converting them into physical action, interacting with other neurons, firing or not firing, and in general maintaining a vast array of physical, electrical and chemical conditions. And a whole lot more. Not bad for a single cell.

What is coordinating all of this intricate behavior? I say, it is proto-mind. A different, perhaps simpler kind of mind than you or I have now, but a kind of mind nonetheless.

What I would like to discuss now is the idea of the evolving mind. It is a feeling and concept that has come to me from many different sources and directions. From personal experience, my studies of the Buddhist teachings, conversations with my teachers and everything else that goes into making an idea. This idea is not explicitly found in the Buddha's teachings, but in my view, it goes along with the doctrine very well. Yet, as the Buddha always admonished, use your own judgment and make up your own mind as to what is true and useful and beneficial. My idea could be wrong.

The duty of the colony

OK, back to the neuron. I say that it is a kind of proto-mind that is coordinating, overseeing, and managing all of that intricate behavior. Definitely not a trivial task. Is this proto-mind conscious? I imagine that it is conscious of its activities and its duty. It is a neuron. A neuron has a job to do as part of a larger whole. A neuron is a part of a colony, part of a larger body. It is not independent. It has to function as a piece of a greater whole.

Eventually this neuron dies, maybe dying with the larger body, maybe before. For the neuron it's death either way. But rebirth is not just for us homo sapiens, it is the rule for all. The proto-mind behind the neuron is then reborn as another cell in another body/colony. Probably as another neuron, after all, it has the right qualifications. So it lives another life, or hundred, or thousand lives as a neuron, in the body of a human, a bear, a worm, or a bird, gathering experience. And, as always, death comes. But from the experience in each life, incremental changes occur in the tiny iceberg of subconscious knowledge ever growing beneath the surface.

This proto-mind traveler also gets reborn as a different kind of colony cell, as its experience allows. A hundred lifetimes as skin. A hundred in the stomach. A thousand in the heart. One life a hair cell and the next a kidney cell, always gaining experience. And over so many lifetimes in the various colony cell-stations our friend masters what needs to be known.

Its iceberg has grown, and it is ready to leave the colony. Our friend is ready to take full control.

Independence

In a glorious moment in our friend's story, it is reborn as an independent single-celled organism. Some simple bacteria, perhaps. Independent and mobile. A young spirit dependant only upon its own wits for its survival. No ectoplasm to bring the food. No friendly red blood cells bringing oxygen. No one to regulate body temperature. Hard work.

There is no colony for our friend to depend on. Proto-mind has evolved to the simplest form of true mind.

Duty drops away and is replaced by a survival instinct which is driven by a happiness/pain polarity. Happiness attracts and pain repels. Avoiding being eaten, enjoying eating. Again, lifetimes come and go, avoiding pain and looking for happiness, experiencing different types of single-celled forms of increasing complexity. And the iceberg grows.

Team leader

The next big milestone that occurs in our friend's evolution is the step from single to multi-celled organism. Here the mind must be powerful enough to organize and manage a group of cells. Our friend is back to the colony, but this time, as the mind organizing the colony. And, as when our friend was a member of the colony, all the cells that make up his/her body are organized by proto-minds, each on their own evolutionary path.

Our friend's mind is no longer confined to a single cell, but is sort of overlaid, or distributed across the cells of the colony, interacting with the proto-minds. The happiness/pain polarity continues as the engine driving development. New tricks are learned to avoid being eaten; new tricks are learned to find food. And now, as a multi-celled life form, gender has become hardwired into the body. Our friend is now a he or a she, and for the physical form to reproduce, these hes and shes must come together. Lifetimes come and go. Our friend passes through many, many different forms – jellyfish, flatworm, insects, vertebrates – slowly growing the iceberg..

When enough knowledge and capability has been amassed, our friend is ready for the most amazing opportunity thus far on his journey, the chance to operate the human form. The chance to get behind the wheel of intention and free will. For the first time, our friend will have the power to amplify his/her intentions throughout the levels of creation, using the amazing mind/brain transducer.

Behind the wheel without a map

At this point our friend's heaven and hell are more or less empty. Prior to mind using the human form, the level of intention is so low that it does not have the power to create any substantial structures in the angelic or hellish realms. Remember, those heavenly palaces and hellish furnaces are created by our own human intention. These structures and forms are built up human lifetime after human lifetime by ourselves.

Now, if you're conscious enough to be reading this book, then it is quite evident (from a Buddhist standpoint) that you have been around for countless lives as a human. You have developed enough so that abstract metaphysics is of interest to you. So, having been human countless times, you and I have hells and heavens of our own creation.

Our friend though, at this point, has a clean slate. And so this next, most important and creative phase of his journey begins. With time and experience his field of knowledge will increase, until he can wisely exercise his intention and free will.

Advice for the new kid

So what sort of advice can we give our friend as he begins the human adventure? The same advice that is suitable for ourselves as well. We should protect ourselves and our mental worlds. First, begin with the Five Precepts – the foundation of human morality. Once the harmlessness of the Five Precepts has become completely integrated and fixed into our worldview and behavior, we will no longer be reborn lower than humanity. Why? Because we will no longer generate hellish tickets. That doesn't mean that we never feel bad or get upset, because we do. It means that we don't get so upset or so angry that we become, momentarily, less than human. With the Five Precepts permanently locked as our baseline, our negative feelings and intentions remain within the human sphere.

And we can move beyond the Five Precepts to cultivate positive states of mind which work to safeguard our Mental Equilibrium.

The Four Ideal States of Mind

Loving-kindness *(Metta)*

Compassion *(Karuna)*

Sympathetic Joy *(Mudita)*

Equanimity *(Upekkha)*

Loving-kindness: Everyone wants to be happy. People love their own lives, and would like to be shown kindness. Thus we should do unto others, giving love to all, and wish all others happiness. And as good begets good, our mental intention of loving-kindness brings happiness to our mental world. We should do our best to make a habit of viewing the world with loving-kindness.

Compassion: Other beings wish to be free from suffering too. We should have compassion for ourselves and all who suffer. If I have compassion, then I would like you, myself, and all others, to be free from suffering. Compassion is good mental habit to adopt.

Sympathetic Joy: In this mental state we appreciate and find joy in other peoples' success, without the least bit of envy. We realize that natural laws are at work and that the person is receiving the fruits of past good action. This is not always easy – for example when a co-worker advances into a position we think that we deserved more. However, the big picture of karma is always fair, and jealousy never brings a good result. We should congratulate them and share in the joy of their success.

Equanimity: This means that when you find yourself in a position where the practice of loving-kindness, compassion, and sympathetic joy cannot be helpful to a specific person or situation, you maintain stability of mind, a nonjudgmental indifference. You neither jump for joy nor let events outside your control break your spirit. You realize that all outward manifestation is subject to the law of change, decay and decomposition. Reality is merely the expression of natural law. It is as it is. Let it be.

These four virtues should be cultivated until they are firmly established in our mental world, and the opposite mental states, such as anger, selfishness, and jealousy, should be abandoned. This is the way to happiness.

Furthermore if we practice mindfulness and become dedicated observers of ourselves and the world around us, we will grow steadily in wisdom. Until finally, our iceberg contains the wisdom and experience and information we need to continue our evolution of mind without the necessity of physical form. Once our knowledge has reached a critical mass, the human game has been played out for us, and we can make another choice. A choice to continue in a state of complete freedom, independent of physical form, beyond this world of opposites, beyond happiness and suffering, beyond birth and death. This is Nirvana.

We are all developing at our own pace. Once we have full knowledge and understanding of our suffering, and the fact that our own placement of false values on objects has led to a clinging that has created our suffering; once we really understand that true and complete freedom from suffering is possible, and we see that there is a way to reach this freedom through self-development and mindfulness; then we will. be ready for our final step in this long journey – the step out of this physical cage.

We will have made a grand journey. We will have passed from pre-proto-mind, to proto-mind, to mind, to the fullest of human mind, and finally to total freedom.

May all beings have a wonderful journey.
May all beings be free from suffering.

Final thoughts

We are all brothers and sisters on an amazing journey
through a constantly changing universe.
Sometimes we feel pain. Sometimes we are happy.

Our own effort and action are the engines of our development.

The laws of nature are rational and can be understood.
All actions have reactions,
and each of us is responsible for all we do.

Being born human is a fantastic opportunity
because we have the enormous creative power
of our intention and free will.

We are our own masters.
We create our own fate, our own heaven and our own hell.
We create by the use of our intention and free will.

Our human mind is always creating.
Our mental environment is our own responsibility.

By practicing harmlessness, compassion and loving-kindness
we cause no harm to ourselves or the world,
thus creating no new negative feedback.

By paying attention, staying mindful, and bravely examining
ourselves and nature, we grow in wisdom.
This wisdom will clean our world.

Ultimate freedom is a reachable goal.

May we all meet again
free from all suffering
and laugh together at the past.

Nibbānaṅ
Paramaṅ
Sukhaṅ

The Three Characteristics

The Buddha taught that all things, both material and non-material, are conditioned states. That is, they come into being due to certain conditions being present. All these conditions are changing. Thus all things come into existence, persist while always changing, and then pass out of existence. Further, the Buddha perceived that every conditioned state, literally all existence, is subject to three characteristics: impermanence, suffering, and non-self.

Impermanence: Everything has a beginning and an end. No *thing* is permanent.

Suffering (conflict, imposed change): All conditioned states are temporary structures subject to suffering, conflict, change imposed upon them.

Non-self: All things are a collection of conditions. We can point to none of these things or conditions and say that is me, that is myself. We can point to an action, but not to the actor.

The Four Noble Truths

The Four Noble Truths, the first teaching the Buddha gave after attaining his own enlightenment, stand in their profundity and simplicity as one of the timeless foundations of Buddhism, for us to return to again and again to deepen our understanding of the situation we find ourselves in, and focus ourselves clearly on the path to freedom. They have been translated many different ways. Here is the basic concept:

One: The truth about suffering, stress, dissatisfaction. Human life exists in time, space, energy and flux where food must be had, breath must be taken, and plans must be made. A place where we are not ultimately in control. We are not even the masters of our own body. It will grow old, get sick and die. All is impermanent. Bodies, families, nations, and planets rise and fall. Joy will come, but it will also go. We should observe and understand the impermanence of all things and the role this plays in our suffering.

Two: There is a cause, a root, at the base of all our feelings of suffering, stress and dissatisfaction. The cause of our suffering is our grasping and clinging, to gain something that we do not have, to hold on to something that is impermanent, or to get away from that which we do not want.

Three: There is freedom from all suffering, all stress and all dissatisfaction. When grasping and clinging come to an end, permanent freedom from suffering is truly possible. It is possible for us to attain this freedom.

Four: There is a path from where we are now to total freedom from suffering. A path to the end of grasping and clinging. It is called the Eight Fold Path. Diligent practice of this path will lead to freedom. Theravada Buddhism is the practice of this path.

The Eightfold Path

The goal of Buddhism is the permanent end to suffering. To reach this goal requires a plan, a path. The Noble Eightfold Path is just that. It is a middle way between the extremes that either deny our physical body or indulge its appetites.

It consists of eight parts, or factors, which are not meant to be followed step by step, one after another, but should be considered part of a single unified path to be practiced simultaneously, to the best of one's ability. Progress in one area will lead to progress in another.

Right Understanding

Right Thought

Right Speech

Right Action

Right Livelihood

Right Effort

Right Mindfulness

Right Concentration

1. **Right Understanding** means a proper understanding, or view, of things the way they are. That is to say, proper understanding of the Four Noble Truths – which includes the Eightfold Path. In this way the Four Noble Truths and the Eightfold Path are nested within each other. Understanding the Four Noble Truths means

    1) understanding our dissatisfaction, stress, and suffering;

    2) that our suffering is ultimately caused by our clinging and craving in an ever-changing, impermanent universe;

    3) that there is a true and permanent end to suffering; and

    4) that the way to reach this end is the Eightfold Path.

2. **Right Thought** has three aspects. The thoughts which we extend to all beings should contain

    1) a kind of selfless detachment – an absence of lust,

    2) benevolence, love, and freedom from ill-will,

    3) harmlessness, non-violence, and free from cruelty.

3. **Right Speech** means speaking what is true, useful and beneficial, pleasant and gentle, timely, friendly and kind. It is deeper and more comprehensive than the Fourth Precept. It means refraining from

    1) telling lies,

    2) backbiting or slander,

    3) harsh, rude, impolite, or abusive language,

    4) frivolous, useless, idle talk or gossip.

4. **Right Action** means refraining from killing, stealing, sexual misconduct, and taking intoxicants. Precepts number One, Two, Three and Five. This is the basis (along with Right Speech), of moral, honorable and peaceful conduct. Right Action involves cultivating loving-kindness, compassion, generosity and self-control.

5. **Right Livelihood** means that one should make one's living in a way that brings no harm to other living beings. Five types of livelihood are to be avoided;
  1) trade in weapons
  2) selling alcohol or intoxicating drugs
  3) trade in poisons
  4) the slaughter of animals
  5) the trade in animal or humans (selling living beings)

6. **Right Effort** is about overcoming obstacles to our development. It has four components focusing on our cultivation of wholesome (useful, beneficial, good) states and our elimination of unwholesome (destructive, unskillful, evil) states. Right Effort is the effort, the exertion, the energetic will
  1) to prevent new unwholesome states from arising.
  2) to get rid of those unwholesome states that have already arisen.
  3) to cause, create, and bring into being new wholesome states that have not yet arisen.
  4) to develop and cultivate and bring to perfection wholesome states which have already arisen.

7. **Right Mindfulness** is about 'being in the moment,' aware of what is going on right now. To practice Right Mindfulness we should try to be aware and attentive with regard to the activities of
  1) the body. Breathing meditation is one method to develop this aspect of mindfulness.
  2) the feelings and sensations. Are they pleasant, unpleasant, or neutral? Watch them appear and disappear.
  3) the mind. Be aware if we are lustful or not, have hatred or not, are deluded or seeing clearly.
  4) ideas, thoughts, mental cooking and conceptions. Watch thoughts appear and disappear. Are they beneficial? Do they match with the truth of nature?

8. **Right Concentration** is a four phase development of mental control through meditative practices.
   1) In phase one we let go of unwholesome mental states (such as lust, worry, ill-will and restlessness) leading to a state of joy and well-being.
   2) In phase two mental activities come to a peaceful rest. Our joy and well-being remain.
   3) In the third phase, the joy recedes, replaced by an alertness and mindfulness.
   4) In the fourth phase all sensations disappear; there is no more joy or sorrow: no division between ourselves and the world; an equanimity and mindful awareness remain.

These eight factors are aimed at developing and perfecting the three aspects of Buddhist training:

Ethical conduct/Morality
Right Speech
Right Action
Right Livelihood

Mental discipline/Concentration
Right Effort
Right Mindfulness
Right Concentration

Wisdom
Right Understanding
Right Thought

Dependent Origination

Buddhism teaches the law of cause and effect. There is no effect without a cause. The principle of Dependent Origination, one of the most profound Buddhist teachings, is a map of sorts, following twelve links of cause and effect, one after another, in both the rising and falling of a moment of thought, and in the cycles of physical rebirth. Each link in the chain causes the next link to occur; without the previous cause, the following effect cannot arise.

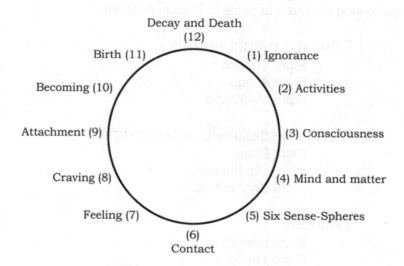

(The diagram on page 52 corresponds to links 6 through 9.)

Publication of this book was made possible by the generous donations of the following people. I wish to thank them all and I am happy in knowing that they shall receive full merit for their actions.

1. Phra Borommathat Doi Suthep Foundation   80,000 Baht
2. Wongvipa Devahastin na Ayudhya   30,000 Baht
3. Surapee Rojanavongse, Amara rattakul, Laliwan Kanchanacharee   23,500 Baht

10,000 Baht
(1) Prof. Dr. Khunying Payom Singhasaneh   (2) Athicha Xanthavanij
(3) Suchin Ratanasiriwilai   (4) Kanokerat Piyanetidham
(5) Varaporn Polla   (6) Duangsmorn-Wanphen-Thanakorn Udomratchatavanich

5,000 Baht
(1) Maneephan Sakteera   (2) Yvan Outrive
(3) Worachun Yujinda   (4) Khanitha Akaranitikul
(5) Suwattana Klongtrakul   (6) Linda Xanthavanij
(7) Satapiya Petcharat

4,000 Baht
(1) Sirinun Piamkulvanit, Chaiyaporn - Thanawan Koonarungsri

3,000 Baht
(1) SanchaiPhamaranon - Ponrawee Ongsinmongkon Phamaranon,
    Siamlung Sae Ung, Pranom Phamaranon
(2) Nirissra Ratanachote - Rikarn Pairashavess
(3) Nuchanart - Pranee Visudhipol   (4) Piyanuch Nuengchamnong

2,000 Baht
(1) Suphanij Nivatavong   (2) Siwarote Siriluck
(3) Srirayab Vinicchykul   (4) David - Pusadee Salisbury
(5) Wathana Bhavilai   (6) Rachada Ruangrote
(7) Sirima Ariyachaipanich   (8) Roongtiwa Patrathiranond
(9) Sunthriya Prabyai   (10) Pimpatchar Boonthittanont
(11) Chularat Chaitiparsana   (12) Ukrit Jirapatrsuntohn, MD

1,600 Baht
(1) Athikom Xanthavanij   (2) Naravadee - Nuttchanon Jivakanunt

1,500 Baht
(1) Worawit - Nechanok - Pattarapa Sukeiam (2) Max Georg Klein, Family

1,000 Baht
(1) Upasika Piengduen Tanasanpipit   (2) Veena Phuachan
(3) Naree Rungpiboon   (4) Wacharee Punwutikorn
(5) Panita Janthapadchothe   (6) Yongyudt-Chalao Supakalin
(7) Vattanee Ngawpitaktham   (8) Kasinee Songjaroen
(9) Nina W.   (10) Paporn Baoprasertkul
(11) Boonpatcharee Phasittisakon   (12) Metha Tuntiwong
(13) Thanu - Pacharanan Naovaratpong   (14) Siriporn Thongtrakul
(15) Wipoo Kumnerddee, MD   (16) Pattamavadee Waranimman
(17) Siriwan Krissanasmit   (18) Pattanee Suchariyasai

500 Baht

(1) Phramaha Amnuai Mahapooñño
(2) Panupong Wangprapa
(3) Watcharapol Kaweewon
(4) Chudsuda Dheerakul
(5) Angkana Maitrisorasan
(6) Nonthida Leklerssiriwong
(7) Gp.Capt. Kitti Tantaobharse
(8) Sqn.Ldr. Jitrakorn Phuthong
(9) Sqn.Ldr. Thongvut Piamanee
(10) Aim-on Nuchdachanun
(11) Monthira Manapitakpong
(12) Palida Jirapathongchai
(13) Tawapak Tiyabhorn
(14) Prach Chulabat
(15) Chatchai Toraksa
(16) anonymous

300 Baht

(1) Komson Boonchumjai, Family
(2) Tippawan Naprasert
(3) Direkporn Parapin
(4) PhongPhan Unmueang
(5) anonymous
(6) anonymous

200 Baht

(1) Phanee Siraprapa
(2) Pavich Piyasirivej
(3) Chaisiri Pantitanonta
(4) Arune Kraisakdawat, Family
(5) Poomjai Pongpanich
(6) Noppadol Prachuabmon
(7) Leekeng Lekwutthikarn
(8) anonymous

100 Baht

(1) Col. Thanat Decha
(2) Paulsilpa Rattanachudech
(3) Anukrit Anukoolsawat
(4) Premsiri Charoenphon
(5) Natwiraya Pansakul
(6) Chansin Chawyong
(7) Phramaha Sane Detna
(8) Taweesak Trisaengrujira
(9) Napaporn Kingrungpet
(10) Prapatsorn Trisaengrujira
(11) Ralita Trisaengrujira
(12) Rapheephan Trisaengrujira
(13) Thotsawat Homganjan, Family
(14) Kittichai Khayhan, Family
(15) Yuparat Wongsa, Family
(16) Thunyaporn Paungpoomkaew, Family
(17) Wattanapong Suttapak
(18) Nutthida Chaiwan
(19) Suruedee Chinthakanan
(20) Aurai Bhavilai
(21) Varunee Kangmaneegul
(22) Pratoomrat Kitghanont
(23) Walaiphan P.Prapasranan
(24) Chokchai Ratsombut
(25) Chuan Supadee
(26) Somboon Patanapreechasathien
(27) Kanitha Chancharoen
(28) Thamnoon Ponpuing
(29) Jirayu Raksuwan
(30) Weena Thammatorn, Parent
(31) Wutthipong - Yupin Chaisaen
(32) Wallapa Techawatchareekul
(33) Wilaiporn Atiya
(34) Natkrita Tantikittichai
(35) Pimonmas Tantikittichai
(36) Kungwan Ruksasat, Family
(37) Nathaya Pongsiriphat
(38-43) 6 anonymous

Extra

Damrong-Chantira Bhavilai, Family (1,009), Ariyajit Dhamarangsri (1,001), Pipat Ruankam (555), Kriangkrai Wongmaleewatana (140), Apichat Thamnitha (125), Wannaporn Duangkhet (50), Wonvarai Techatit (20), Sompong Plienjaisook (20)

Paid for cover

Upasika Piengduen Tanasanpipit (1,000), Anukrit Anukoolsawat (100), Komson Boonchumjai (100), Tippawan Naprasert (100), Thotsawat Homganjan (100)